A garden where children continue to challenge themselves

There is a story full enough

Even today and tomorrow

I am sure to keep on born forever

子ども達が自分自身に挑み続ける園庭

そこにはあふれるほどの物語が

今日も明日もその先も

きっとずっと生まれ続ける

As travelers in the world, a good start from a playgarden makes the journey more fulfilling.

The months and days are the wayfarers of a hundred generations, and the years that come and go are also travelers. (translated by Hiroaki Sato)

In the Edo Period (1603-1868) when Genroku Culture flourished, the Japanese poet Matsuo Basho (1644-1694) wrote this in the introduction to his *Oku no Hosomichi* (The Narrow Road to the Deep North). He said, "Our life is like a journey in this tempestuous period. If we think our individual life is a moment of the long history of humanity, we can feel calm and peaceful." This was quoted from a poem written by Li Bai (701-762) in the Tang dynasty period in China.

If we apply this poem to the modern world, travelers include vessel and aircraft crews, people traveling around the world for business or pleasure, and everyone else who lives on this earth.

For this reason, we need to seriously consider the future of the earth, follow the Paris Agreement adopted by the 21st session of the conference of the Parties (COP 21) to the United Nations Framework Convention on Climate Change, and nurture the spirit of love for the earth by stopping our destruction of the environment.

Meanwhile, based on progress in the study of the brain supported by the development of artificial intelligence (AI), it is understood that exercise utilizing our five sense are most important for the intellectual development. Having a playgarden surrounded by nature, including animals, insects and plants, is desirable for developing the five senses.

In other words, a desirable playgarden has an ever-changing environment of weather, temperature, animals, and plants that is a space where children can play peacefully with nature.

Playgarden equipment with some height differences promotes a wide range of movements that help children to naturally recognize that gravity may cause risk. This enables them to avoid serious accidents and nurtures their physical strength through active play.
To guarantee such an environment in which children can start their life leads to the happiness of all those living and traveling on the earth.

January 2018
Shigeharu Kumao
President, ANEBY CO., LTD.

人は地球を住処(すみか)とする旅人
ならば　人生のよいスタートは園庭から始めよう

月日は百代(はくたい)の過客(かかく)にして 行(ゆ)きかふ年も 又旅人 也
(月日は永遠の旅人のようなものであり、毎年、来ては去る年も、また旅人のようなものである)

　江戸時代、元禄文化の華やかなりし頃、俳人 芭蕉(1644-1694)は「おくのほそ道」の序文で、このように語りかけています。これは「この激動の時代、『人生は旅』であり、自分の一生は人間の長い歴史の中で『一瞬を生きる旅人』だと思えば、『心の平和』が得られる」という、中国の唐時代を生きた詩人 李白(701-762)の漢詩より引用された一文です。
　このことを現代風に例えるならば、船舶や航空機の乗組員、ビジネスや観光で世界を巡る人々はもとより、この地球上で生きているすべての人が、地球を住処とする旅人であると考えられます。
　だからこそ今、地球の未来について深く考えるならば、太古から存在する地球にほんの一瞬しか住まない旅人である私たちは、COP21(気候変動枠組条約第21回締約国会議)のパリ協定で宣言されていることを最低限実行していかなければならないし、同時に、今の地球環境をこれ以上破壊することなく、「地球を愛する心」を育んでいかなければならないとの思いに至ります。

　一方、乳幼児教育の分野では、AI(人工知能)の開発で脳の研究が飛躍的に進み、現在、知能の発達には「五感を使った運動」が最も重要な遊びであると、理解されるようになりました。そして乳幼児が五感のすべてを使って行動するには、動物・植物など多くの生きものに触れ合い、遊ぶことができる自然環境が整った園庭が理想です。
　つまり理想的な園庭には季節の移ろいや、刻々と変化する天候や気温、子ども達の意思とは関係なく動き続ける動物、日々、成長する植物など変転極まりない環境があり、それは正(まさ)しく乳幼児が動植物と共生できる空間、「『心の平和』の庭」なのです。
　さらにこの他に高低差があり、さまざまな動きが生まれる遊具が設置されていれば、「危険に最も影響する重力」というものへの認識が生まれ、大きな事故に遭うことなく、活発な遊びをたくさん経験し、複雑な動きへの応用力が育まれていきます。

　そして乳幼児がこのような園庭から、人生を始められる環境を保証することこそが、地球を住処とし、その愛する地球の隅々まで旅する私たち人類すべてに、幸せをもたらすことになるのです。

平成30年1月
株式会社アネビー
代表取締役　熊尾重治

Need for Playgarden Design

Aneby proposes comfortable playgarden designs that fully utilize the natural environment.

In Germany and other countries in northern Europe, many kindergartens do not have buildings. These are called forest kindergartens. The concept is that experiences in early childhood are very important for future growth. Children's experiences at nursery schools and kindergartens have a significant influence on their development. If they are surrounded by a wealth of nature, they can accumulate experience that is desirable for the nurturing of creativity. However, due to the unstable weather and population concentration in urban areas, it is difficult to find forests like those that are in northern Europe near nursery schools and kindergartens in Japan. Fortunately, many Japanese schools have a playgarden, and we thought it would be possible to provide the desirable environment for children with playgarden design.

We believe our mission is to design playgardens suitable for the environment of individual schools to nurture fitness and sensibility.

Extract from the Approaches to Kindergarten Design and Specifications

We should think of a kindergarten playground as a classroom without a roof. (***snip***) It is a place to experience and learn where children develop the basic life habits, knowledge and abilities that they need for healthy growth. In other words, it is the place to experience education regarding health, society, nature, language, music and rhythm, and painting. With this in mind, there should be no differences among playground, classroom, and gym. (III. Playground Design, 1. Characteristics of Playground, 2. Playgrounds at Kindergartens)

Space for fixed equipment such as swings and slides, places for trees and plants, and flat square spaces are essential for kindergarten playgrounds. These must also be designed for consistency from the viewpoint of children's activities, teaching, and management. In other words, it is desirable that a kindergarten playground consist of three different areas: a play area with fixed equipment, a flat area, and an area that is natural, like a forest, hill or river. In other words, places for equipment, places to play with friends, and places to play with nature. (III. Playground Design, 2. Playground Designing, 1. Factors that Determine Designs, B. Forms)

Source: Approaches to Kindergarten Design and Specifications. Edited by Japan Kindergarten Facility Council. 1957. P.22-30.
Provided by AOKI Early-childhood Education Research (AEER)

Designing playgardens where children can develop physical fitness and motivation

The basis of the physical fitness and motivation that each child needs for the future is developed during childhood. Preparing a playgarden environment where children can enjoy play utilizing their entire body and build the habit of trying until their goal is achieved is the responsibility of adults. We should blend nature with a well-designed playgarden to increase the value of their activities.

Playgarden equipment that promotes mutual learning

Most nursery schools and kindergartens provide group education. Teachers give instructions to children, which is insufficient to develop children's motivation to try challenging tasks, to increase their courage to fight against bullying and unfairness, and to develop leadership skills.

These abilities are usually nurtured while children play freely among their peers. It is essential, therefore, to have playgarden equipment that encourages children to try, compete, and cooperate with friends.

Designing a playgarden that nurtures sensibility

The essential ability of Japanese children is thought to be sensibility that leads to creativity. In Sweden, preschools are called daytime homes. Homes consist of buildings and gardens, and they think that gardens are essential to developing mental strength and sensibility. It is desirable to design beautiful playgardens fully utilizing nature and equipment that develop imagination and creativity.

HAGS 🇸🇪

*"Hags takes play seriously" is the guiding principle for this Swedish company. Founded in 1948, the practicality and durability of HAGS playground equipment has helped it grow into a company that exports to 70 countries in Europe and other spots around the globe. Specifications for the materials used in every piece of playground equipment demand the highest standards, and individual parts can be combined freely for different purposes. The parts can be adjusted to accommodate conditions, and extension and alteration are always possible. To create the circumstances that allow children to play as naturally as if were in nature and encourage them to try new skills, HAGS continues to insist on the highest standards as it develops prototypes to ensure improvements that realize safe and secure functions.

※HAGS（ハグス）は1948年に設立。「HAGS takes play seriously（我々は遊びを真剣にとらえている）」が信条で、福祉国家スウェーデンを本拠に、ヨーロッパを中心に70か国以上へ輸出され、その遊具の実用性・耐久性は世界で実証されている。遊具を構成する基本部材の規格が決まっており、「遊び」によって組合せは無限。設置条件に対応し、植栽との融合、増設・組み替えもできる。また子ども達が自然の中で見せる遊びの「動き」を再現し、「本物の挑戦」を用意するため、試作・試用を繰り返して機能達成したものだけが製品化されている。

『園庭設計』の必要性

アネビーは遊具（HAGS※）を基本に、自然を取り入れた『園庭設計』で、
子ども達のための遊び環境づくりを提案しています。

北欧やドイツでは、園舎をもっていない『森の幼稚園』がたくさんつくられています。その理由は幼児期の「原体験」が子どもの「育ち」にとって、とても重要だからです。子どもにとっての「初めて」は、敏感な感覚で多くのことを体感できる貴重な経験であり、また自然の中で遊ぶことで、創造力を育む豊かな体験が積み重ねられ、その後の人格形成に大きく影響すると考えられています。

しかしながら日本では、変化しやすい天候や都市部の人口集中などによって、幼稚園・保育園の近くに北欧のような「森」を求めることは非常に困難です。しかし幸いなことに多くの幼稚園・保育園には「園庭」という遊び環境があります。

だから今、子ども達に必要とされる「運動能力」と「感性」を育むために求められているのは、「自然の森」に負けない『園庭設計』による「遊び環境」をつくり上げることであると考えています。

「幼稚園のつくり方と設置基準の解説」抜粋

「(前略)幼稚園の運動場は『屋根のない保育室』というように考えるべきである。(中略)こどもの生活学習経験の場であって、そこであらゆる必要な能力や知識・理解・態度などの基礎的な芽生えや基本的な習慣を身につけていくのである。いいかえれば、健康・社会・自然・言語・音楽リズム・絵画製作の教育内容の全領域にわたって望ましい経験を得ていく場所である。したがって、運動場と保育室や遊戯室などの園舎との間には何等価値的な差別はないのであり、また差別をつけてはならないのである。」
(Ⅲ. 運動場のつくり方　1.運動場の性格　2.幼稚園の運動場 より)

「幼稚園の運動場はぶらんこ・すべり台等の固定運動用具を設備した場所、樹木や草の繁った土地、および平坦な広場は欠くことができない。しかもこれらは、幼児の活動の面、指導の面、管理の面からそれぞれ中心的なまとまりをもつようにすることが必要である。すなわち、主として固定運動用具を使って遊ぶ場所、広い平坦な場所、起伏のある林、小山、小川等のある場所、いいかえれば、人工的な機械・器具を使っての遊び、人間関係を中心とした遊び、自然を中心とした遊びの3つの場所から構成されることが望ましい。」
(Ⅲ. 運動場のつくり方　2.運動場の施設計画　1.施設計画を決定する要因　B.形態　より)

出典：「幼稚園のつくり方と設置基準の解説」全国幼稚園施設協議会編、
　　　昭和32年(1957年)、p22-30　資料提供：AEER青木幼児教育研究所

「運動能力」と「挑戦意欲」が獲得できる園庭づくり

子ども達が生涯を過ごすために必要な「運動能力」と「挑戦意欲」は、園庭で遊ぶ幼児期にその基礎部分が構築されてしまいます。だからこそこの幼児期に十分に身体を使って遊ぶこと、そしてできるまで挑戦し続ける習慣が身につく「園庭環境を整えること」が、私たち大人の責任です。つまり自然遊びの要素を上手に取り入れ、さらに「遊びの価値」を向上させる魅力的な遊具を取り入れた「園庭づくり」が必要です。

子ども同士で学び合うための遊具施設

今、幼稚園・保育園のほとんどが一斉保育です。先生の指示に従うことが中心となるため、自主的な行動力が備わるには不十分になり、言葉だけでは伝わらない「困難なことに挑戦する意欲」や、「いじめや不正と闘う勇気やリーダーシップ」を身につけることが難しいのです。

しかしそれらは「大人に監視されていない子ども同士の集団で、自由に遊ぶこと」によって育まれます。だから子ども同士で競争や挑戦をしたり、隠れ家で空想物語を協調して演じることができる遊具が不可欠です。

「感性」を育む園庭づくり

今、日本の子ども達に必要不可欠な能力は、独創性が重視される「感性」だと言われています。北欧の国スウェーデンでは、幼稚園・保育園をプレスクール(事前学校)とし、「昼間の家庭」と呼びます。「家庭」とは「家」と「庭」から成り立ち、「庭」は「心や感性」を育むためになくてはならないものと考えられています。つまり「庭」にはできる限りの自然を取り入れ、色彩感覚の優れた「想像と創造する力」を育てる美しいデザインの遊具を取り入れた園庭が理想です。

Five Basic Principles of Playgarden Development

1. Safety
It is essential to consider safety, which ensures an environment in which children can concentrate on activities. Aneby conforms to EN-1176 and 1177, the European safety standards for playgarden equipment. These standards have a long history and have achieved good results. In accordance with Accident Analysis Stage (See page 168), we eliminate hazards from the playgarden environment by designing a structure and environment that prevent accidents while encouraging children to explore new challenges.

2. Functionality
Safe playgarden equipment does not always mean good playgarden equipment. Equipment supports growth, so it should include the function of improving physical development. In addition to safety, therefore, it is very important to confirm that the equipment is attractive enough to encourage children to try, that it is sufficiently durable for repeated daily use, and that it can be extended through additions.

3. Design & Creativity
It is equally important that the equipment's structure and location make it easy for children to imagine stories, and that its design promotes the development of creativity. It is also important that the equipment is in harmony with the surrounding natural environment. What adults think is beautiful, children also think is beautiful.

4. Quality
Activities create the culture of the school and the playgarden provides the space to learn. Therefore, it is important that the playgarden has appropriate materials and textures. It is also important that the playgarden equipment conforms to ISO 9001, is easy to maintain and that parts are easily replaceable when worn or broken.

5. Environmental adaptability
We ensure that equipment materials are free of substances that may be harmful if touched or ingested. We also confirm that the materials do not produce hazardous substances in the event of flood or fire, and that they are environmentally friendly.

Seven Elements Required for Playgarden Development

To ensure that the attractiveness of the playgarden is sufficient to motivate children to explore new challenges, the following seven elements are essential:

1. Imitability
Enabling children to join in play by allowing them to imitate what others do.

2. Contingency
Enabling a variety of new movements and the pleasure of discovering new things.

3. Competitiveness
Enabling children to make and follow rules, and enjoy the process of reaching goals.

4. Risk
Enabling challenging activities and the pleasure of achievement.

5. Privacy & Singularity
Enabling space for children to be alone or with friends without direct supervision.

6. Circularity & Repeatability
Enabling routes and mechanisms that allow children to repeat what they enjoy.

7. Dizziness & Fascination
Has an element to temporarily numb the senses.

遊び環境づくりの5つの基本

1. 安全性
安全性は子ども達が本気で「遊び込む」ためにはどうしても欠かすことができません。そのため私たちは、遊具の安全について歴史と実績のあるヨーロッパ安全規格「EN-1176・1177」に準拠しています。そして「事故分析ステージ（p.168参照）」を基に、遊びの環境から「ハザード（あってはならない危険）」を取り除き、重大な事故を発生させない構造と環境を設計し、毎日の遊びで挑戦と「リスク（挑戦する危険）」がより効果的に機能することを目指しています。

2. 機能性
「安全＝よい遊具」というわけではありません。遊具は子ども達の「育ち」を支えるもので、平常時では使わない身体機能を鍛える構成であることが必要です。そのため子どもにとって挑戦意欲を刺激される魅力があるか、毎日繰り返し遊んでもレベルアップに耐えられるか、機能を増設・拡張することができるかはとても大切です。

3. デザイン・創造性
子ども達が空想（ファンタジー）や物語の世界を描きやすい場所や構造をもち、創造性を育むことができる美しいデザインであること。そして周りの自然環境と調和していることも大切です。私たち大人が見た時に美しく感じるものは、子ども達が見ても同じように美しく感じることができます。

4. 品質
子ども達の遊びは「園の文化」をつくり、園庭は「学び合う」場。だからそれにふさわしい材質や手触りでつくられていることが大切です。そして遊具のどこが壊れてもメンテナンスが可能で、国際品質保証規格の「ISO9001」に定められたサービスを履行できることが重要です。

5. 環境適応性
肌にふれたり、なめたりしても健康に問題はないか。万が一、水没や火災にあっても、有毒なものが発生しないか。また安いという理由だけで、地球環境を壊す原料をむやみに用いていないかについても、きちんと考えています。

遊び環境づくりに必要な7つの要素

「遊び場」において、子ども達にとっては何が魅力的で、挑戦意欲を刺激されるのかを7つの要素で考えます。

1. 模倣性
これまでの記憶や友達の様子を見て真似て、一緒に行動できること。

2. 偶然性
予期しない動きが発生し、変化に富んでいること。また新しい発見の喜びがあること。

3. 競争性
友達とルールを決めて行動したり、できるまでの過程を楽しんだりできること。

4. リスク性
勇気をもって試みるものがあること。試みた結果、達成の喜びがあること。

5. 秘密性・特異性
大人に監視されないで、ひとり、または友達と静かに過ごす場所があること。

6. 回遊性・反復性
気に入ったことを飽きるまで繰り返し行うことのできる、ルートや仕掛けがあること。

7. めまい・陶酔性
一時的に知覚を麻痺させる要素があること。

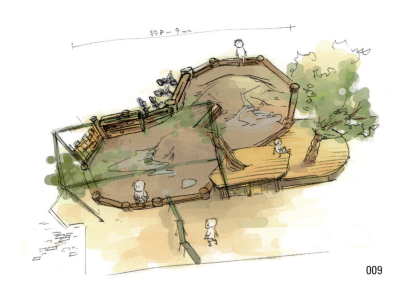

■ INDEX

Prologue ·· 004

Need for Playgarden Design ································ 006

[Chapter I] Creating a Playgarden — 019

■ Kawawa Nursery School [Yokohama City, Kanagawa Prefecture] ···· 020

The only playgarden designed to nurture potential, ···· 020
and consider the growth of each child.

Kawawa Nursery School Playgarden ···················· 020

Extracted from "*Tsubuyaki* – Words from Children," ···· 035
Memories of Kawawa Nursery School for Graduating Children

Kawawa Nursery School Events ··························· 036

Thinking and playing ··· 044
Interview with Shintaro Terada, Principal

■ Omori Minori Kindergarten [Ota-ku, Tokyo] ················ 046

At a corner of the city where we feel nature's breeze with our entire body. ···· 047
An ever-changing forest watches over individual children's growth.
Interview with Mitsunori Fujisawa (Principal) and Hiroko Fujisawa (Vice-principal)

Athletic Square ··· 048

Surprise Mountain and Sunshine Deck ················· 052

Twin Peaks and Ninja Mountain ························· 056

Green Square ··· 060

Planting ··· 064

Certified Center for Early Childhood Education, Fukui Kosei Kindergarten [Fukui City, Fukui Prefecture] — 066

Imagining the swings in 10 years. Becoming a kindergarten in the forest. — 066
Setsuko Oyanagi, Vice-principal

A wonderful childrearing challenge – Commemorating the 50th Anniversary — 068

From Ninja Village to Sand Pool – Separating Zones for Growth Stage – — 069

Grow with Nature – The playgarden will also grow into a forest someday – — 070

Playgarden Layout — 070

Enjoji Nursery School [Yusui-cho, Aira-gun, Kagoshima Prefecture] — 078

Water brings smiles to the children's faces — 078
– A playgarden filled with water and fun activities –
Masashi Ishigami, Principal

Two water sources support activities that contribute to mental development — 080
– Sakurajima –
– Small Jewel Deck & Gacha Pump –

A secure space for small children – Deck & Entrance Slope – — 082

Children's Kingdom full of enjoyment — 082

Kodatsuno Zenrinkan Kodomoen [Kanazawa City, Ishikara Prefecture] — 088

A playgarden where children feel the pleasure of being surrounded by — 088
soil, water, trees, flowers, and sunshine
Keiko Yoshida, Principal

Sources of Challenge and Achievement – Two Hills and Three Towers – — 090

Pleasure of Harvest and Involvement with Nature – Harvesting and Food Education – — 091

Different ways of playing and achieving goals — 092

Specialists Engaged in Playgarden Development – Playgarden Design Institute – — 098

[Chapter II] The Variety of Playgarden Layouts ········· 099

Our playgarden is a small world of nature — 100

Rissho Koseikai Kosei Ikujien/ Suginami-ku, Tokyo — 100

Saga Kindergarten/ Kyoto City, Kyoto Prefecture — 104

Seishin Soyo Kindergarten/ Sagamihara City, Kanagawa Prefecture — 106

HAGS Equipment — 108

Suminoe Kindergarten/ Osaka City, Osaka Prefecture — 108

Matsumoto Kindergarten/ Edogawa-ku, Tokyo — 112

Meisai Kindergarten/ Niiza City, Saitama Prefecture — 114

Challenges await the children — 116

Yamanashi Gakuin Elementary School/ Kofu City, Yamanashi Prefecture — 116

Showa Women's University Showa Elementary School/ Setagaya-ku, Tokyo — 120

Ozora Himawari Nursery School/ Yokohama City, Kanagawa Prefecture — 124

Comfortable and challenging — 126

Certified Center for Early Childhood Education, Kahoru Nursery School/ — 126
Kofu City, Yamanashi Prefecture

Hinamori Nursery School/ Nichinan City, Miyazaki Prefecture — 130

Kataoka no Sato Nursery School/ Kitakatsuragi-gun, Nara Prefecture — 132

The slope is also a fun place to play — 134

Higashi Taiten Nursery School/ Higashi-Murayama City, Tokyo — 134

Narita Nursery School/ Narita City, Chiba Prefecture — 138

Specialists Engaged in Playgarden Development – Manufacturing Department – ⋯⋯⋯⋯ 140

[Chapter III] Structuring the Playgarden ⸺ 141

Elements that motivate activity ⸺⸺⸺ 142

▨ Hill ⋯⋯⋯⋯ 143	▩ Stone Wall & Ninja Hut ⋯⋯⋯ 155
▩ Jabu Jabu Pond (Gacha Pump) ⋯ 145	▩ Planting & Pergola ⋯⋯⋯ 156
▩ Biotope ⋯⋯⋯ 147	▩ Planting Plan ⋯⋯⋯ 158
▩ Sand Pool & Daimore ⋯⋯ 148	▩ SKY Shades ⋯⋯⋯ 162
▩ Deck (Sunshine, Small Jewel, etc.) ⋯ 149	▩ Random Fence ⋯⋯⋯ 163
▩ Tree Deck ⋯⋯⋯ 150	▩ Small Hut & Michikusa Deck ⋯⋯ 163
▩ Cradle Swing ⋯⋯⋯ 151	▩ Water Play Cottage ⋯⋯ 164
▩ Aerial Cable ⋯⋯⋯ 152	▩ Raised-Floor-Style Hut for Mud Ball Making ⋯ 164
▩ Trampoline ⋯⋯⋯ 153	▩ The Net Sea ⋯⋯⋯ 165
▩ Go-kart Course ⋯⋯⋯ 154	▩ Bridge of Dreams ⋯⋯⋯ 165

Opening ceremony ⸺⸺⸺⸺⸺ 166

Technical data ⸺⸺⸺⸺⸺ 167

Creating a safe environment for children's activities ⸺⸺⸺ 168

Epilogue ⸺⸺⸺⸺ 174

■目次

はじめに	004
園庭設計の必要性	006

【第1章】 園庭を創造する　019

■ 川和保育園　神奈川県横浜市　020

子どもの力を信じ、 その育ちを真剣に考える ここだけに在る「子ども達の園庭」	020
川和保育園の遊び場	020
子どもたちの「つぶやき」― 卒園文集より	035
川和保育園の行事	036
自分で考え、自分で遊べ 子どもたち 園長 寺田信太郎先生のお話から	044

■ 大森みのり幼稚園　東京都大田区　046

緑の風を全身に感じる都会の一角 そこは子どもの育ちを見守り、変化し続ける豊かな森 園長 藤澤光徳先生、副園長 藤澤普子先生のお話から	047
アスレチック広場	048
びっくり山とこもれびデッキ	052
ふたつ山と忍者山	056
みどりの広場	060
植栽	064

■ 認定こども園 福井佼成幼稚園 福井県福井市 066

10年後のブランコを夢見る、目指すは「森の幼稚園」 066
教頭 大栁世津子先生

「園庭保育」のための50周年の挑戦 068

にんじゃのさとから、さらさら砂場まで 　―成長に合わせたゾーン分け― 069

自然と共に…いつかは森に… 　―五感で楽しむ植栽― 070

見わたす限りの「遊び場」 070

■ 円乗寺保育園 鹿児島県姶良郡湧水町 078

豊かな水は子ども達の笑顔も豊かに「水と遊びの湧き出る園庭」 078
園長 石神正之先生

ふたつの水源が子ども達の遊びと心を潤す 080
―さくらじま―
―小さな勾玉デッキ&ガチャポンプ―

小さい子達の安心スペース 　―縁側デッキとエントランススロープ― 082

楽しさ湧き出る子どもの王国 082

■ 小立野善隣館こども園 石川県金沢市 088

土や水、樹木や花の香、陽の光の中で「生きる喜び」を実感できる遊び場 088
園長 吉田敬子先生

挑戦と達成の源 　―2つの築山と3つのタワー― 090

実りの喜び、自然とのかかわり 　―収穫と食育― 091

遊びも挑戦も十人十色 092

遊び場をつくる人たち 　―園庭デザイン研究所― 098

【第2章】さまざまな園庭　099

園庭は里山　100

立正佼成会附属 佼成育子園　東京都杉並区　100

嵯峨幼稚園　京都府京都市　104

誠心相陽幼稚園　神奈川県相模原市　106

シンボルタワーHAGS　108

住の江幼稚園　大阪府大阪市　108

松本幼稚園　東京都江戸川区　112

明彩幼稚園　埼玉県新座市　114

挑戦も回遊する　116

山梨学院小学校　山梨県甲府市　116

昭和女子大学附属 昭和小学校　東京都世田谷区　120

おおぞらひまわり保育園　神奈川県横浜市　124

憩いと挑戦　126

認定こども園 かほる保育園　山梨県甲府市　126

ひなもり保育園　宮崎県日南市　130

片岡の里保育園　奈良県北葛城郡　132

斜面も遊び場　134

東たいてん保育園　東京都東村山市　134

成田保育園　千葉県成田市　138

遊び場をつくる人たち　―製造部― ……………………………………………… 140

【第3章】園庭を組み立てる —— **141**

さまざまな「やってみたい」を生み出す要素 …………………………… 142

■築山 ……………………… 143

■じゃぶじゃぶ池（ガチャポンプ）…… 145

■ビオトープ ……………… 147

■砂場＆だいもれ ………… 148

■デッキ …………………… 149

■ツリーデッキ …………… 150

■ゆりかごスウィング …… 151

■空中ケーブル …………… 152

■トランポリン …………… 153

■ゴーカートコース ……… 154

■石垣・忍者小屋 ………… 155

■植栽・パーゴラ ………… 156

■植栽計画 ………………… 158

■スカイシェード ………… 162

■ランダムフェンス ……… 163

■小屋＆デッキ …………… 163

■水遊び小屋 ……………… 164

■高床式どろだんご小屋 … 164

■ネットの海 ……………… 165

■夢のかけ橋 ……………… 165

お披露目式 ……………………………………………………………………… 166

技術資料 ……………………………………………………………………… 167

安全な遊び環境づくり ………………………………………………………… 168

あとがき ………………………………………………………………………… 174

【第1章】
園庭を創造する

[Chapter I]

Creating a Playgarden

「遊ぶことは学ぶこと。」
保育でよくとりあげられるこの言葉から、
みなさんはどんな遊び環境を想像するでしょうか？
ここでは『園庭を創造する』というテーマで、
子ども達が歓喜の声を響かせ、自然にふれ、仲間をつくり、
経験という成長の基礎を築いている園庭を5つ紹介します。
この5つの園庭には子ども達が望む、
本当にたくさんの「やってみたい」がつまっています。
だからページをめくる間、自分が子どもになって
思い切り遊んでいるところを想像してみてください。
きっとみなさんの園庭を創造するきっかけが眠っているはずです。

"Playing is learning."

This phrase is often heard in discussions of childcare. What type of play environment does this phrase bring to mind ?

Here we introduce five actual playgardens. Surrounded by nature, children play happily with their friends as they gain experience that contributes to their development.

These five attractive playgardens encourage children to explore and grow.

As you turn each page, please imagine yourself as a child on the playgarden.

You may discover keys to creating your own.

川和保育園 神奈川県横浜市
Kawawa Nursery School [Yokohama City, Kanagawa Prefecture]

子どもの力を信じ、
その育ちを真剣に考える
ここだけに在る「子ども達の園庭」

　園に一歩、足を踏み入れると、大きな木々に包まれた「子ども達の庭」が視界いっぱいに迫ってきます。次に見えるのは、そこかしこで思い思いに遊ぶたくさんの子ども達の姿。その顔は真剣だったり、笑っていたり、泣きそうだったり、怒っていたり、眠そうだったり、「豊かな」という言葉が本当にしっくり感じられるほど千差万別です。

　ここは横浜の郊外、園長の寺田先生を中心に先生方と保護者の方々が一体となって、約30年以上をかけてつくり上げた「子ども達の園庭」。1,600㎡の敷地には卒園までに遊びつくせないほどの遊具と、季節の訪れや自然の営みを告げてくれる木々や草花に満たされています。

　だから子ども達はこの二つとない園庭で、全身を使い夢中になって遊びに挑戦したり、想いのままに自分の作品や居場所をつくることに、一生懸命で充実した「遊びの時間」を過ごしています。やがて子ども達はそれぞれの早さで、それぞれの個性を育て、ここを巣立っていきます。

The only playgarden designed to nurture potential, and consider the growth of each child.

As you enter Kawawa Nursery School, the large trees surrounding the playgarden catch your eye. You then notice children using their imagination as they play freely. Some are concentrating intently, some are laughing, some are crying, some are angry, and some are sleepy. Each shows different expressions and feelings.
This is a suburb of Yokohama. Under the initiative of Kawawa Nursery School's director Terada, over the past 30 years, successive teachers and parents have worked together to create the playgarden. Situated on 1,600 m² of land, the playgarden is filled with equipment that students will eventually outgrow, and trees and flowers that teach them about nature and seasonal changes.
This great environment encourages the children to move their bodies, use their creativity, and develop their own playtime activities. Each child's individuality grows as their bodies and minds develop during their time here.

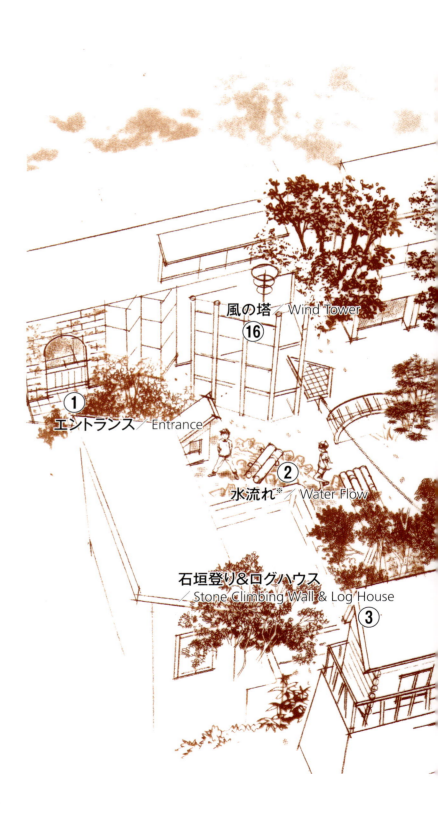

川和保育園の遊び場

※アネビーでは植物に囲まれて水遊びができるビオトープを、上流が「水源」、中流が「水流れ」、下流が「じゃぶじゃぶ池」という三要素に分けて名称付けしている。/ *Aneby classifies biotopes where children can play with water surrounded by plants into three elements: Upstream headwater; Midstream water flow; and Downstream Jabu Jabu Pond.

【第1章】園庭を創造する

川和保育園の遊び場
Kawawa Nursery School Playgarden

①エントランス／Entrance
始まりを予感させる物語性のある入口。
Its atmosphere makes everyone feel as if they've stepped into the beginning of a story.

②水流れ／Water Flow

エントランスからの水流れは爽やかに子ども達を誘います。
The refreshing flow of water from the entrance entices the children.

③石垣登り&ログハウス／Stone Climbing Wall & Log House

子ども達の挑戦意欲を誘う石垣登り。てっぺんにはログハウス、遊びの先にも遊びが用意されています。
The stone climbing wall encourages children to try their best. A log house awaits them at the top of the wall.

④グラウンド／Ground
「タイヤのついた乗り物で人にぶつかってはいけません」がルール。
It's against the rules to bump into others with the karts.

⑤回転塔／Rotating Tower
くるくるくるくる。子ども達はびっくりするほどの高速回転でもへっちゃらです。
Going round and round. Children love to whirl around.

【第1章】園庭を創造する

⑥おとぎの家／Fairyland House

お父さん達の卒業制作遊具で、2009年の卒園文集のタイトルである「ふってもはれても」をコンセプトにした屋根が特徴の遊具です。

The fathers of graduating children built the fairyland house. The roof design reflects ideas taken from a collection of essays written by children who graduated in 2009.

⑦山砂砂場／Mountain Sand

園に6つある砂場のひとつ。水をためて泥風呂にする子が続出しています。

This is one of six sand pools at the nursery school. The children enjoy filling them with water to make mud baths.

⑧大工コーナー／Carpenter Corner

本物の工具を使って、自由に作品をつくることができます。

Children are free to use their imagination to make things with real tools.

⑨ だいもれ／Daimore

砂でダムをつくって、水をためたら一気に決壊させる大胆な遊びが「だいもれ」の由来。
この遊びは山砂の立体砂場という環境と、子ども達の共同作業により、完成されます。

Daimore is an exciting activity. Children make a sand dam, fill it up with water, and then destroy the dam. This activity integrates a multi-level sand pool and cooperative effort.

⑩ **だいもれタワー** / Daimore Tower

地上5階のタワーには普通の階段がありません。子ども達は頂上制覇に自分の総力を傾けます。
The five-level tower does not have a traditional staircase. Children use their energy and wits to reach the top.

⑪ スモーランド／Smaland

3階建てのHAGSのオリジナル遊具。2階にはトランポリン、1階には可愛い住人がいます。

Smaland is a three-level playgarden structure sold by HAGS. The 2nd level features a trampoline, and a cute animal is living on the 1st level.

⑫ 空飛ぶ船／Flying Ship

ヤナギの木を支えとしたこの船に乗船するにはロープ伝いで幹をよじ登るか、登り棒で上へ。縄梯子は降りるとき専用。

This ship rests on a willow tree, and children board using a rope to climb up the tree or shimmy up poles. The rope ladder is for coming down.

⑬ **ツリーハウス**／Tree House

イチョウの大木につくられた、これもお父さん達の卒業制作遊具。登るためには握力、腹筋力、背筋力、つま先までの脚の筋力、バランス感覚、そして勇気と意志力が備わっていることが必須です。

This tree house was also made by fathers of graduating students. It takes a strong grip, abdomen, back and legs, a sense of balance, courage, and drive.

⑭ たき火／Bonfire

寒い日には温まったり、仲間同士で団らんや工作をしたり、焼き芋や干し柿で食育できる癒しの遊び場です。

On chilly days, the children gather here for warmth, conversation and creative activities, and learn how to cook sweet potatoes and dried persimmons.

⑮ こもれびデッキ／Sunshine Deck

ケヤキが大きな枝を伸ばし、夏は茂った葉が木陰をつくり、秋には落ち葉がデッキを彩り、冬の梢からは暖かい日差しがふりそそぎます。

A zelkova stretches its large branches to the middle of the deck. The foliage provides shade in summer, fallen leaves give color to the deck in autumn, and the bright, warm sun shines through the treetop onto the deck in winter.

⑯風の塔／Wind Tower

3階には空中ロープウェイの発射台があり、挑戦への葛藤と勇気が子ども達を待っています。
The launch point for the sky ropeway is on the 3rd level, giving children a chance to develop their confidence for new challenges.

制約があるからこその環境
遊び空間の広さは横だけでなく、縦への展開も重要。登った充実感とてっぺんからの別世界のような景色を獲得できる。

Turning limits into potential
It is important to provide children with not only wider, but also higher spaces to play. They feel fulfillment after reaching the tops of the playgarden structures, and are rewarded with a grand view that gives them completely different perspective from what they see from the ground.

さいしょは のぼれないなあっていう
きもちだったんだけど
だんだん のぼりたいなあっていう
きもちになって
そしたら
のぼれたんだ

でもね おちるって
おもったときより
ちょうせんしようって
おもったときのほうが
ドキドキした

いいてんきって しってる?
あったかくて
ぴかん ぴかんって
ひかってる ひの こと

「やりたい!」にいつでも挑戦
挑戦するのも、できなくて引き返すのも子どもが自分で選ぶ。でも自分で決めた挑戦ができた喜びはこの上ない達成感となる。

Trying and succeeding
It is the child that chooses to try or give up. Success creates a sense of fulfillment and heightened confidence.

あした あさからあそぶんだ
あしたも あしたもあそぶんだ
あしたのあしたのあしたも
ずーっとね

保育の中心は「園庭」
子ども達は保育園のほとんどの時間を園庭で過ごし、来る日も来る日も飽きもせず夢中になって遊んでいる。

The playgarden is the heart of childcare
Children spend most of their time at nursery school on the playgarden. They pass day after day playing happily.

原体験を心と体の原点に
子ども時代の思い出は人の心にとどまり続ける。それと同時に遊びから得た経験は体に刻み込まれる。

Providing formative experiences for healthy mental and physical growth
The memories of our youth remain with us forever, and our experiences on the playgarden are an important source of those memories.

こころは
そだてるもんじゃない
どんどん どんどん
どーんどん
おおきくなって
いっちゃうものだ

経験することでしか学べない
ドキドキヒヤリの怖さがルールを守る意味を理解させ、経験として積み重ねるからこそ、生涯、自身を守る「身のこなし」となる。

Children learn only from what they experience
Feeling fear in situations teaches the importance of following rules. The accumulation of such experience teaches children how to protect themselves.

子どもたちの「つぶやき」 川和保育園 卒園文集より抜粋／Extracted from "Tsubuyaki – Words from Children," Memories of Kawawa Nursery School for Graduating Children

川和保育園の行事
Kawawa Nursery School Events

じゃぶじゃぶ池 / Jabu Jabu Pond

夏の川和保育園では園庭の真ん中にジャングルジムを据えた大きな大きなじゃぶじゃぶ池が出現します。一本橋を渡ってジャングル島へ行ったり、カヌーで乗り入れたり、子ども達の壮大な水遊びが展開されています。

A large pond equipped with a jungle gym is installed in the center of Kawana Nursery School's playgarden in summer.
Children reach Jungle Island by canoe or by crossing a bridge. They enjoy water activities here.

ゴーカート／Go-kart

川和の運動会／Kawawa's Sports Festival

もちろんこの園庭でも運動会が開催されます。ゴーカートやSケン*、タイヤ運びレースで日頃の成果を発表します。

They also have a sports festival. Children show their families what they have learned here through their day-to-day activities. They ride on go-karts, compete for an S-shaped base*, and race carrying a tire.

左／タイヤ運びレース。右／Sケン*／
(Left) The tire race (Right) Competing for the S-shape base*

川和の竹馬／Kawawa Stilts

子ども達が自らつくる竹馬。年長さんには2月に竹馬レースが待っており、小さい子の憧れでもあります。また卒園式にも園生活の集大成として、それぞれの上達ぶりで在園児と保護者がつくる花道を誇らしげに歩いていきます。

Children make their own stilts. The older children run in a stilt race in February. Smaller children look forward to their chance to race like them.
At the graduation ceremony, the older children walk on the stilts through a flower path made by the smaller children and parents with the pride that comes from having achieved a wide range of development goals.

※地面に大きくSの字を描き、円状になる部分をそれぞれの陣地とし、敵陣にある「宝」を奪い合う昔ながらのゲーム。「宝守り」「陣守り」などの役目を作戦会議によって決め、S字の開いた「門」から「宝とり」が片足ケンケンで出撃。敵陣の「宝」を自陣に持ち帰ったら勝利。役割分担が重要なカギとなり、チームプレイで競い合う／*After drawing a large S-shape on the ground, two groups use the opposite circular areas as their base in this game, and they try to take the other group's treasure. At the tactical meeting, members decide each person's part, such as treasure guards or ground guards. First, the treasure guards hop out on one foot to attack the other group's area from the open section of the S-shape. The first group to capture a treasure from the other group and return with it to their area wins. Assigning roles is the key to winning with good teamwork.

川和の大山ごま／ Kawawa Oyama Top Spinning

園長先生も交えて、本気の競い合いが展開される園庭には「じゅみょっこ、じゅみょっこ」と唱える声がこだまします。上達してきたら園長先生の前で 5 回連続のこま回しを披露。成功したら「マイごま」がもらえます。

With the principal joining in the fun, the top spinning competition fills the playgarden with shouts of joy. As their skill improves, they proudly show the principal. When they succeed in spinning the top 5 times, they win a top of their own.

川和のバザー／ Kawawa Bazaar

この「子ども達の園庭」は年間、約800万円の借地代を父母の会の「小さな力も大きな愛に」というテーマのもと、バザーの寄付で半分近くを補っています。多くの人の想いに支えられたこの園庭で、子ども達は今日も育ちの日々を過ごしています。

This Kawawa Nursery School Playgarden is on land rented at a cost of approximately 8 million yen per year. Approximately half of the rent is paid through profits from a bazaar organized by the parents' association. The theme of the bazaar is "Helping children grow."
Support from everyone involved in the nursery school community ensures the children learn and grow in a safe and secure environment.

お父さん達の「卒園制作遊具」 / Dad's Graduation Gift - Play Equipment

毎日子ども達の挑戦を受け止めているこの園の多くの遊具は、卒園していく子ども達のお父さんが協力し合い園に残していく作品です。頑丈で組み立てと解体が自由自在なHAGSの部材を利用して、子ども達に合った遊具を残したいというリクエストに応え、アネビーの園庭設計デザイナーが基本設計をし、度重なる打合せの上、組み立て作業へと進行。20数名のお父さん達が参加し、無事完成へ。お披露目初日は子ども達が遊具に鈴なりになるほど喜ばれました。

Most of the equipment on this playgarden has been donated by the fathers of graduating students. The fathers wanted to leave something for future students and decided upon equipment sold by HAGS, equipment that can be assembled and disassembled easily. In response to their request, playgarden designers at ANEBY Co., Ltd. discussed designs. With the participation of more than 20 fathers, the equipment was assembled. On the day of the opening ceremony, children were so excited about the new equipment and played on it to their heart's desire.

鯉のぼり 端午の節句／Carp-shaped streamers, Boy's festival

自分で考え、自分で遊べ　子どもたち

園長　寺田信太郎先生のお話から

　子ども達にとって「園庭」がいかに大切かということを、私たちはもっと知って、もっと考えて、いかに子ども達の成長に不可欠な「環境づくり」をするかが重要だと思います。幼児期の子ども達は人間の一生のうちで最も多くのことを学び、多くのことを感じ、その先の成長の基礎をどれだけ増やせるかという大切な時期。だから子ども達が自らやりたいと思った遊びを、伸び伸びと、思い切り、そしてたっぷりとできることが一番だと考えます。

　例えば一つに「身のこなし」。これはさまざまな遊びをする中で、楽しいだけではなく、登りたい、飛んでみたいという未知なる世界への欲求を叶えたいと思う反面、落ちるかもしれないという「恐れ」を感じながらも、何度も何度も試行錯誤して挑戦していくことがその子の経験値＝身のこなしとなります。またそれは体の育ちだけではなく、達成できた喜びによって勇敢さや大胆さ、粘り強さなどの心の育ちにもつながっていくのだと思います。そんな川和保育園では、先生方にも「見守る」という大切な役目があります。例えば遊具や木に登る子ども達が必ず自分の力で登るのを見守り、大人が絶対に手を出したり、手伝ってはいけないというルールがあります。つまり子どもの握力や、姿勢をコントロールする力は一人ひとり異なり、それぞれの「ドキドキとヒヤリ」を繰り返し経験することで自分にとっての「危険」を考え、乗り越える力を身につける。これは言葉で他人が教えることはとても難しいからです。でもここで身につけた力は生涯、子ども達が身を守る大きな力になるからこそ、大変重要になると思います。

　もう一つは「ルールを守る」こと。川和保育園の園庭では0歳児から5歳児までが交じり合って遊んでいます。だからここは友達に譲ろうかとか、ここは赤ちゃんが来るから注意しようとか、子ども同士の関わり合いがとても自然にできています。それは自分の遊びから学んだ怖さや危険をきちんと理解して、ルールを守ることの本当の意味を理解しているからです。それは他人に対しての思いやりや社会規範の理解、そして人と人とのつながりを築き、大切にできることにもつながっていくのではないかと思います。

　最後の一つは「環境の変化」。園庭には四季の移ろいがあり、晴れたり、風が吹いたり、朝や夕方、そして葉が茂ったり、落葉したり、花が咲いたり、実がなったりといった同じ場所でも目まぐるしいと感じるくらいさまざまな変化をしています。そして子ども達はその変化に新しい発見をし、遊びを発展させ、その過程も楽しんでいます。子どもにとって「変化するもの」は興味深く、保育室の中だけでは感じることができない貴重な体験なのです。

　子ども達にとって「園庭」は、育ちのための大切な大切な居場所です。

Thinking and playing
Interview with Shintaro Terada, Principal

We need to understand that the playgarden is a precious and important experience for all children; and it is essential for us to provide the ideal environment for growth. What children learn during their preschool years provides the essential foundation for their future mental, physical and emotional growth. During this important time of their lives, children should be free to explore and grow in directions that interest them. This, I believe, is the most important aspect of childhood education.

For example, children develop agility through trial and error. As they try activities that they have not yet experienced, they sometimes fail, and sometimes feel fear. Repeating such experience many times, the children come to learn how to use their bodies. This not only leads to physical development, but also psychological growth in areas such as confidence, courage, and resilience. Teachers at Kawawa Nursery School have the important role of watching over the activities of the individual children without interfering in them. For example, when a child climbs on play equipment or trees, they watch the children but avoid stepping in to help them. The reason for this is that the ability to negotiate obstacles and the chance to overcome fear is different for each child, and watchful observation enables each child to learn to handle situations. We do not learn these important lessons from others. We learn by being allowed to work through them on our own. Once learned in this natural way, the experience becomes the foundation for safe and confident movement that continues throughout our lives.

We also focus on the importance of following rules. At Kawawa Nursery School, children aged from several months to 5 years have places on the playgarden. During this time, they learn naturally to care for others in accordance with the situation. For example, they learn to exercise care where infants are present, and show consideration for others. They learn this by learning about and understanding dangerous situations and the importance of following rules. This, I believe, leads to the development of concern for others, an understanding of social norms, and the establishment of trusting relationships with others.

We also provide the opportunity for children to notice changes in their environment. They see daily and seasonal changes on the playgarden. Sometimes it's sunny, and sometimes it's windy. They also see changes between morning and evening. Trees turn green, flowers bloom, leaves fall, and fruit grows. At the same time, they see lots of other changes throughout the year. Children discover the new, develop activities, and enjoy the process. Change is always interesting to children, and it provides precious experience that cannot be provided inside.

The playgarden is an important place for children.

上／現在の園庭
下／以前の園庭
(Above) Current playgarden
(Below) Previous playgarden

【第1章】園庭を創造する

「見守る」ということ

園長先生を始め、川和保育園の先生方は「見守る」ということに大きな意義をもち、子ども達を信じ、子ども達からも信じてくれているという関係を築きあげています。だからここで育ち巣立っていった卒園生が大人になっても「保育園時代は楽しかった」と鮮明な記憶とともに、その充実した時間を笑顔で語ってくれるのです。

To "watch over"

All the teachers at Kawawa Nursery School understand the significance of watching over children. They know that children place their trust in their teachers. After they grow up, they all say, "It was very fun and exciting playing at this nursery school," with smiles on their faces.

大森みのり幼稚園 東京都大田区
Omori Minori Kindergarten [Ota-ku, Tokyo]

緑の風を全身に感じる都会の一角
そこは子どもの育ちを見守り、変化し続ける豊かな森

園長 藤澤光徳先生、副園長 藤澤普子先生のお話から

「たくさん体を動かすことができて、たくさん感性を磨くことのできる、子ども達が目を輝かせる場所にするために、熱意と工夫で、もっともっと園舎も園庭も、子ども達の好奇心を満足させる遊び場にしたい」といつも考えている園長先生。

そして幼稚園のあらゆるスペースが、保育にどう活用できるかが検討され、大型木製遊具を中心とした「アスレチック広場」、水と砂に思う存分ふれられる「びっくり山とこもれびデッキ」、新たな身のこなしを経験できる「ふたつ山と忍者山」、芝の緑が美しい「みどりの広場」と、たくさんの素敵な遊び場が生まれてきました。

最初に手掛けた創立50周年を記念してできた「アスレチック広場」は、『もったいない』の精神で既存の遊具に木のぬくもりを増やしてリニューアルし、屋根を付けて隠れ家をつくり、「鳥の巣」を経由した吊り橋と「山のぼりスロープ」の完成で、園舎とつながった大きな回遊性と挑戦意欲をかきたてる大立体遊空間になりました。他の園庭もつくり込むほどに、それぞれの特徴が際立ってきています。そしてどの園庭でも、子ども達はびっくりするほどの挑戦意欲をもち、いろんな遊びを創造し、自分のやりたいことと居場所を見つけられた笑顔でいっぱいです。

さらに「自分自身も園庭の緑に癒される」と園長先生が語られているとおり、シンボルとなる大きな大きなイチョウの木を始め、多くの木々と草花、そしてさまざまな種類の実りが表現する四季の変化によって彩られ、そこに暮らすものすべてに潤いを与えています。

大森みのり幼稚園の門は、一歩くぐると都会の喧騒が消え、子ども達が「体はたくましく、感性は鋭く、頭脳は賢く」育つ場所への入り口です。

At a corner of the city where we feel nature's breeze with our entire body.
An ever-changing forest watches over individual children's growth.

Interview with Mitsunori Fujisawa (Principal) and Hiroko Fujisawa (Vice-principal)

Principal Fujisawa is constantly considering improvements to the playgarden and school building. He said, "I want to create a playgarden where children can move their bodies freely, develop their sensitivities, and be excited about being outside. Our school should be a place that satisfies the children's curiosity."

They considered the entire school site with an eye toward ideal use for the children's development. Through discussions, they designed attractive spots such as the Athletic Square, which features large wooden equipment, Surprise Mountain & Sunshine Deck, where children enjoy playing with water and sand, Twin Peaks & Ninja Mountain, where children can experience new ways of moving their bodies, and Green Square with its beautiful green lawn.

Their first project was Athletic Square, which commemorated the school's 50th anniversary. Reusing existing equipment, they added wooden material and placed a roof to make a hideout. They also made a suspension bridge via a bird's nest, and a mountain climbing slope, which creates a large circuit connected to the school building, to encourage the children to explore and grow. Other spots have become distinctive as they were improved. The common thread in the design is that it encourages the children to explore the new, create a wide variety of activities, and feel the joy of discovery.

As the principal said, "I am also calmed by the verdure of the playgarden," there are many trees such as a large symbolic gingko tree, flowers, plants, and fruit in the playgarden. They show the children and teachers the beauty of the seasonal changes and create a comfortable environment.

When we enter the gate of Omori Minori Kindergarten, we are separated from the noise of the big city and nestled in an oasis where children can exercise, develop their sensitivities, and grow.

園舎と遊具のつながりは学びと遊びの一体感を生み出す
Integration of learning and play through the connection of the school building and playgarden equipment

アスレチック広場／Athletic Square

トランポリン／Trampoline

屋根裏部屋／Attic

山のぼりスロープ／Mountain Climbing Slope

鳥の巣／Bird's Nest

【第1章】園庭を創造する

「アスレチック広場」ができるまで／Background of the Athletic Square

以前の園庭：既存の鉄製遊具／Former Playgarden: Existing iron playgarden equipment

木製の要素を取り入れてリニューアル／Remodeling with the incorporation of wooden elements.

屋根裏部屋を追加／Adding an attic.

園舎とつながり、回遊性のある大きな遊びの空間ができた／Connected to the garden building, a great circuit of playgarden activities is created.

土や水や風、草木や木々や実り、そしていろんな生きものとふれあう場所
Encounter soil, water, wind, plants, trees, fruit, and many forms of life

びっくり山とこもれびデッキ／Surprise Mountain and Sunshine Deck

「今の子は整備されたところしか歩いていないことが多いでしょ。だからバランスを崩したり、ぬかるみに足をとられたり、滑り落ちそうになってヒヤリとする、そういう微妙な身体感覚の体験をすることが、小さい子ども達にとっては本当に大切なことだと思うの」と語るのは副園長先生。

山砂をたっぷり盛り、ガチャポンプで水流れをつくり出すこの砂山では、地面の凹凸に合わせた柔軟な身のこなしを鍛え、掘る・埋める・形を変えるなどの新しい遊びを発想し、発見している子ども達。その時のびっくりした時の感性を大切にし、遊び込んでほしいという想いから「びっくり山」と名付けられました。

Vice-principal Hiroko Fujisawa said, " Children growing in urban environments have few opportunities to experience nature, opportunities to develop their strength and agility through playtime activities."
At this sand mountain, water flows from the Gacha Pump and many forms of life can be seen. Children develop physical agility by negotiating the irregular surface of the ground, discover new activities such as digging and molding shapes. This play spot was named " Surprise Mountain." It is a place where children can experience the feeling of surprise and excitement as they play to their heart's content.

ランダムフェンスとこもれびデッキ／Random Fence and Sunshine Deck

大きなサクラの木の下には、こもれびが踊るデッキがあります。ここはフェンスにも植物が添えられ、子ども達の憩いの場となっています。

Sunshine deck is under a large cherry tree. Children gather here to relax surrounded by fences covered with greenery.

ガチャポンプ／Gacha pump

ビオトープ／Biotope

春、カエルの産卵とオタマジャクシ。夏、サンショにはアゲハ蝶の幼虫とその羽化、さらにクスノキにはアオスジアゲハやシオカラトンボ。秋はカマキリと冬眠前のカエル。そして冬、池に張る氷。池とその周りの木々が静かに生きものを育んでいます。

Frogs lay eggs, and tadpoles emerge in the spring. We see swallowtail worms on Japanese pepper trees, and Graphium sarpedon and dragonflies on camphor trees in the summer. We see praying mantis and frogs before hibernation in autumn; and we see the ice that covers the pond in winter. The pond and surrounding trees nurture many forms of life.

大イチョウとサクラ ／ Great Ginkgo and Cherry Trees

大田区の保護樹木である2本の木。この園のシンボルであるイチョウは、アスレチック広場とびっくり山の真ん中にあり、デッキのサクラの木とともに、子ども達に季節の移り変わりを告げています。

The great ginkgo and cherry trees are protected by Ota Ward. The great gingko tree, the symbol of the kindergarten, grows in the middle of Athletic Square and Surprise Mountain. It shows seasonal changes to the children.

「びっくり山」ができるまで ／ Background of Surprise Mountain

以前の園庭：のびのびと遊べる空間のためにプールを移設／Former Playgarden: Relocating the pool to create a space where the children can play freely.

UniMiniと土管トンネルなど配置／Installation of UniMini and soil tunnel, etc.

山砂を増量／Increasing mountain sand.

さまざまな植栽とともに、ガチャポンプ・築山・登り木を設置／Installation of the Gacha pump, hills and climbing trees with a wide variety of plants.

【第1章】園庭を創造する

この植物であふれた里山には野性的な遊びが今か今かと待っている
Nature activities await children in this area filled with plants

ふたつ山と忍者山／Twin Peaks and Ninja Mountain

　大きく枝を広げた木々や、さまざまな花や実りであふれたコースをゴーカートに乗って疾走する子ども達の顔は、みな爽快感にあふれています。コースの真ん中にはハンモックや太鼓橋があって、それぞれの「やりたい」に心ゆくまで応えてくれます。またわくわくするほど、子ども達の挑戦意欲を引き出す忍者山には、両手をかけ、裸足で足場を探しながら全身を使って登る石垣と、制覇したものだけが体験できる忍者小屋が待っています。原体験を体験した子ども達は、心も体もたくましく、そして自然の変化を感じ、五感を研ぎ澄ましていきます。

Children riding on go-karts look so happy running the course filled with trees whose branches stretch out and a wide variety of flowers and fruit. In the middle of the course, there is a hammock and arched bridge that the excited children play on. Ninja mountain also attracts the children. It encourages them to climb. Ninja Mountain features a stone wall that challenges the children to identify foot- and handholds, and a Ninja hut on the top where those who have successfully climbed the stone wall can enter. Experiencing the achievement, children become mentally and physically more confident, feel the changes in nature, and develop their sensitivities.

太鼓橋の向こうには富士山が／Mt. Fuji is behind the bridge.

【第1章】園庭を創造する

忍者山と忍者小屋／Ninja Mountain and Ninja Hut

空中ケーブル／Aerial Cable
園庭の端から端を横切る長くて迫力満点のこの空中ケーブルに、2歳児までもが挑戦します。
This aerial cable is long and crosses the playgarden from one edge to the other. Even the two-year old children try this thrilling ride.

【第1章】園庭を創造する

「ふたつ山」ができるまで／ Background of the Twin Peaks

工事前の空き地／ Vacant ground before the start of construction

第一期工事 サイクルロード完成／ The 1st phase of construction – Completion of a cycling road

駐車場だった場所は、約5年をかけて自然豊かな里山になった
A parking lot was made into a natural miniature satoyama over a period of about 5 years.

059

緑の眩しいこの園庭には小さい子ども達の遊びが生まれる
Small children are comfortable playing on this playgarden full of greenery

みどりの広場／Green Square

　緑の芝に覆われたさわやかな風と木々に包まれたこの園庭は、小さな子ども達の「初めて」が安心して体験できるようにつくられています。砂場にはふたがあり、使わない時には安らぎの場所にもなり、遊具も登る・滑る・揺れる・もぐるなどいろんな身のこなしを体験できます。

Covered by a green lawn and surrounded by trees and refreshing breezes, this playgarden was made to give small children a safe and secure environment for their first experience in nature. The sandbox is covered with a lid. When it is not used, the covered sandbox can be used for relaxation. Small children can also experience climbing, sliding, swinging, and burrowing.

小さな子用の遊具／Playgarden Equipment for Smaller Children

【第1章】園庭を創造する

ふたつきの砂場／Sandbox with a Lid

063

大森みのりの木とふれ合い、木と学び、木と生きる
Playing, learning, and living with trees at Omori Minori Kindergarten

植栽／Planting

ブドウ／Grapes　フジ／Wisteria　イチジク／Fig　ナツミカン／Citrus Natsudaidai　クリ／Chestnut　アケビ／Akebi　ツワブキ／Tsuwabuki

モモ／Peach　リンゴ／Apple　ウメ／Plum

胸いっぱいに緑の香を感じてほしい
We hope the children take the greenery into their senses

【第1章】園庭を創造する

園児下駄箱では季節の緑が迎えてくれる／
Seasonal greenery greets you in the kindergarten shopping bag.

右／ランダムフェンスと花壇：園の顔にもなる看板とその周辺も自然でいっぱいに。通りかかる方にも園の気持ちが伝わる。左／以前の入り口／(Right) Random fences and flower beds: Signs and its surroundings are full of nature. The feeling of the garden is transmitted to passersby. (Left) Previous entrance

「この門をくぐる時、子ども達が胸いっぱいになるくらい緑の香を感じてくれたらいいなぁ」と園長先生。その言葉通りに豊かさを湛えた大森みのりの自然は、きっと子ども達の成長に大きな実りを与えてくれるに違いありません。

The principal said, "I hope the children take the greenery into their senses when they enter this gate." The wealth of nature at Omori Minori Kindergarten provides the perfect environment for growth.

認定こども園 福井佼成幼稚園 福井県福井市
Certified Center for Early Childhood Education, Fukui Kosei Kindergarten [Fukui City, Fukui Prefecture]

10年後のブランコを夢見る、目指すは「森の幼稚園」

教頭　大栁世津子先生

　どの公園でも危険が取り除かれて遊びの幅がなくなっているからか、この園庭の開放日にはたくさんの親子が訪れ、通りがかりの子どもからも「遊びたいなぁ」という声をたくさんいただきます。元々、園庭遊びを変えたいと考える前園長が、HAGS社の遊具を気に入り、導入園をいくつも見学。それまでの園庭遊びとの違いに驚き、さらに自然遊びを考えていた時に川和保育園と出会い、自分の園の風土とやり方で自然とふれあう園庭づくりを園の50周年の事業として始めました。園庭で遊ぶことは

**Imagining the swings in 10 years.
Becoming a kindergarten in the forest.**
Setsuko Oyanagi, Vice-principal

After learning and growing through a full range of activities that build their confidence and strength, the children want to show their parents what they can do during open house. Looking to change the quality of playgarden activities, the former principal was very interested in HAGS equipment, and visited other kindergartens that had installed it. The principal

単に遊んでいるという放任した状況ではなく、子どもの成長に重要かつ充実感があり、園庭もひとつの保育ツール・教育環境として保育の重要な環境のひとつとして位置づける「園庭保育」を実現したいという想いからでした。

お披露目初日は築山がつぶれるくらい子ども達が登っていてびっくりしましたが、園庭は年齢ごとのゾーン分けのおかげで全園児が一斉に出ても遊びが混まないし、大きい子の遊びがすぐ隣にあって学びやすいと思います。またルール作りも子ども自身がどう考え、解決するかをじっくり待って、広まっていくのを見守り、園の「気づき、考え、行動する子」に沿って実現できました。今の課題は一年を経て挑戦する子が非常に増えた反面、先生方が解決策を教えたくなる「慣れ」をどう引き締め直して「見守る」ことを続けるかです。また一気に導入したおかげで子ども達の伸び具合のスピードが速すぎたので、今後どう挑戦意欲を高めていくかですね。じゃぶじゃぶ池は大活躍で、今年の夏に期間限定で飛込みもOKにして満足するまで遊ばせたんですよ。おかげで秋になるとむやみに濡れずに遊べるTPOが身につきました。またビオトープにオタマジャクシを放して園庭中がいろんな種類のカエルでいっぱいに。子ども達は大喜びで身近な自然を楽しむ良いきっかけでした。植栽も四季を楽しみ、散る散らない、香る、色が変わる、花が咲く、実がなるなどにこだわった多彩な木々です。カリンやブルーベリーで食育の経験もさせたいですね。

目指すは「森の幼稚園」。10年、20年後には大きな茂みの中で子ども達が遊び、大きくなった木にブランコが揺れる風景を夢見ています。

was very surprised at the difference he saw between traditional playgarden activities and the activities that HAGS made possible. The principal also came to know about Kawawa Nursery School when he was searching for ways to incorporate nature into playgarden activities. As one of the commemorative projects for the kindergarten's 50th anniversary, he started making plans that utilized the school's existing structure and systems for a new playgarden where children could feel and experience nature. Feeling that the children should not simply play in the playgarden, the principal wanted to create an important educational environment that effectively supported growth.

While the grounds were teeming with happy children on opening day, the layout was divided into several zones for each age group so that none of the equipment was crowded; and smaller children could watch and learn what the older children were doing right next to their equipment. Teachers could also observe the children to see how they made rules, identified and solved problems by themselves after they had been taught the principle of the school, "Foster children who can notice, think and act." While the children attempt increasingly complex activities this year, teachers encourage them to think for themselves by refraining from giving immediate instructions. By implementing all the equipment at one time, the children quickly learned and developed skills. This makes it easier for the teachers to continue encouraging them to reach ever higher goals. Jabu Jabu Pond is very successful. We limited the period this summer and gave them the opportunity jump into the pond and play. This allowed them to learn to play without getting wet in autumn. We also left tadpoles in the biotope, which created a playgarden filled with a wide variety of frogs. The children were so happy about the chance to enjoy nature. We also planted a wide variety of trees that show the change of the seasons. Some are evergreen and some are deciduous. Some are fragrant, change colors, bloom, and produce fruit. From now, we want them to harvest and cook quinces and blueberries.

We want this nursery school to be like a forest. I imagine this playgarden in 10 or 20 years as a place where children play under large trees with luxuriant foliage, and I see the swings on the trees with children riding on them.

【第1章】園庭を創造する

福井佼成幼稚園の先生方:広い園庭を見守る先生方は、とてもパワフル/Teachers at Fukui Kosei Kindergarten: They nurture the children as they watch them play.

「園庭保育」のための50周年の挑戦
A wonderful childrearing challenge – Commemorating the 50th Anniversary

園舎から遊具へと子ども達が我先にと向かって行く／Children rush from the kindergarten building to the equipment on the playgarden.

　子ども達は子ども達自身で望み、考えて遊ぶ。それは成長に「遊びが必要」だと子ども達自身が知っているから。ではそのために大人には何ができるだろう？　50周年を迎えた福井佼成幼稚園では園庭を一つの保育ツールと考え、その環境を整えるためにたくさんの試みをつめ込みました。

Children have their own desires, and they think and play along with those desires. This is because children instinctively know that playing is essential for their growth. At the 50th anniversary of the school, Fukui Kosei Kindergarten decided to improve the playgarden environment considering it to be an important educational tool.

にんじゃのさとから、さらさら砂場まで —成長に合わせたゾーン分け—
From Ninja Village to Sand Pool – Separating Zones for Growth Stage –

【第1章】園庭を創造する

園舎から見て園庭の右側から左側に向かって、年齢層の高い子ども達がその成長に合った挑戦ができるように遊具が配置されています。だから園児全員が園庭に出ても遊びが混むところもなく、またそれぞれの大きい子達の挑戦を隣で見て、小さい子達も挑戦するため著しいスピードでの成長がみられました。

Looking right to left from the side of the kindergarten building, we can see that the equipment is arranged to match the different stages of growth. Therefore, all children can play without crowding at any one spot. In addition, smaller children can see what older children are doing close up, which accelerates growth.

自然と共に…いつかは森に… ―五感で楽しむ植栽―
Grow with Nature – The playgarden will also grow into a forest someday –

おひさまガーデン／Ohisama Garden

平面図（上／雑草園、下／畑）
ground plan [(Above) Weed Garden, (Below) Vegetable Garden]

見わたす限りの「遊び場」
Playgarden Layout

① 赤の塔／Red Tower
② 緑の塔／Green Tower
③ にんじゃのさと／Ninja Village
★ おひさまガーデン／Ohisama Garden

スイカズラ／Honey Suckle　　レンギョウ／Golden Bell Flower　　ハギ／Bush Clover　　雑草園／Weed Garden　　畑／Vegetable Garden

【第1章】園庭を創造する

　園庭のあらゆる場所に、びっくりするぐらい多くの種類の植物が、一つひとつ名札をつけられて植えられています。また、園庭のそばにはサツマイモやミニトマト、オクラなど実りのある畑とさまざまな雑草を観察し、触れることのできる雑草園ができました。自然にふれ、愛でる。卒園し、大きくなっても、ひとつでも名前を憶えていてくれたらと願っています。そしていつかは森になり、大きな木に揺れるブランコに子ども達の歓声があがるといいですね。

Different kinds of plants are growing everywhere on the playgarden, and their names are attached to them so the children can learn. Near the playgarden, they grow sweet potatoes, okra and cherry tomatoes in one area and a wide variety of plants in another. Here the children come to love nature. These plants will form a forest, and in the forest, the happy and cheerful voices of children riding on swings under large trees will fill the air.

森の砦／Forest Fortress ④
築山／Hill
じゃぶじゃぶ池／Jabu Jabu Pond ⑤⑥
UniMini ベクシー／UniMini Bexy ⑦
憩いの場／Rest Area、ビオトープ／Biotope ⑧⑨

①赤の塔／Red Tower

HAGS社の遊具を存分に楽しめる「赤の塔」は、リノベーションの遊具も加えていろんなルートで頂上までの挑戦ができます。てっぺんまで登ったご褒美はスリル満点のチューブスライド。

Red Tower features HAGS equipment. Adding renovated equipment allows children to try a variety of routes to the top. After reaching the top, they can enjoy a thrilling tube slide.

赤の塔から緑の塔を望む／Green Tower seen from Red Tower.

この塔の中にはトランポリンも。飛んで跳ねての感覚は子ども達に大人気／The tower also has a trampoline inside. Jumping and hopping are very popular among children.

②緑の塔／Green Tower

フジが茂るパーゴラとデッキを備えた「緑の塔」は、憩いの空間であり、
大きな遊具へ挑戦するための準備ステップです。

Green Tower has a deck and a pergola covered with thick wisteria to provide a space for relaxation, and room for larger equipment planned for the future.

赤の塔へ向けて、大移動。揺れても傾いてもへっちゃら／Moving toward Red Tower together. They are happy when it swings and inclines.

③にんじゃのさと／Ninja Village

「にんじゃのさと」は入口に仕掛けがあって、普段はお兄さんお姉さんしか入れない。でも小さい子達が憧れのまなざしで覗きにくる姿がよく見られます。

Entry to Ninja Village requires a little trick that only the older children have figured out. Smaller children often come to watch with a look of admiration.

手足を思う存分使って登る、降りる／Climb up and down using their hands and feet.

木のトンネルを抜ける爽快感に何度でも／The refreshing feeling of going through the wooden tunnel makes the children want to try again and again.

④森の砦／Forest Fortress

小さい子のごっこ遊びから、手足を思い通りに動かすための経験もできる「森の砦」は、眺めも抜群。

Forest Fortress provides chances for smaller children to enjoy a wide range of activities. The view from the top is also great.

⑤築山／Hill

築山は登り方も降り方も、みんな千差万別。プレイターフで安全性と景観を両立しました。

Everyone has a different way of climbing up and down the hill. They get a great view, and the play turf ensures safety.

⑥じゃぶじゃぶ池／Jabu Jabu Pond

水とたわむれる子ども達はどの子も真剣で、満面の笑顔。夏はもちろん、冬でも大人気です。

Children are very intent when it comes to playing with water. They have big smiles on their faces.
It is very popular not only in summer, but also in winter.

⑦ UniMini ベクシー／UniMini Bexy

小さい子にも挑戦と自然と憩いの場を。大きい子がいないので安心して過ごせます。
This is only for small children. The secure equipment provides a safe environment to play in nature.

⑧ 憩いの場／Rest Area　　　　⑨ ビオトープ／Biotope

【第1章】園庭を創造する

円乗寺保育園 鹿児島県姶良郡湧水町
Enjoji Nursery School [Yusui-cho, Aira-gun, Kagoshima Prefecture]

豊かな水は子ども達の笑顔も豊かに「水と遊びの湧き出る園庭」

園長　石神正之先生

　子ども達が自分達から、自分の好きなように「遊び」を展開していけるような「子どもの楽園」をつくりたいというのがきっかけでした。ちょうど遊具の老朽化で次をどうするかを考えていた時に、園舎の裏に2つの井戸がある土地があったこと。また川和保育園を見学して「こんな保育園があるんだ」ってカルチャーショックをうけたこともあり、それが子ども時代に、子どもにしか生み出せない文化である「遊び」がとことんできる園庭づくりへと発展していきました。

Water brings smiles to the children's faces
– A playgarden filled with water and fun activities –
Masashi Ishigami, Principal

We wanted to make a paradise for children where they can create and expand their activities as they please. That was the beginning of this nice playgarden. At that time, the school buildings and equipment were deteriorated and we needed to think about what to do. There was also land in the back of the school that had two wells. We also visited Kawawa Nursery

そして今回は保育の観点から、一緒に想いを共有して園庭づくりをしてもらったことで、わざと整地せずデコボコや斜面にしたり、子ども目線での発想やアイデアをもらったり。また元々あった柿の木の周りに、どうビオトープや「かきやま」をつくろうか話をして、こちらの想いを実現してもらったことが一番良かったと思います。

園庭が完成してまず、川和保育園の寺田園長から学んだ「登れる力のある子はちゃんと慎重に降りるよ、信じてあげればいい。変に手伝うとかえって危ない。小さい怪我を繰り返しながら大きな怪我を防ぐから」というお話を先生方にし、どういう見守り体制にするかを十分話し合いました。だから、今まで上から転げ落ちたりする子どもは全くないし、最近では先生方も「子ども達はしっかり分かっている」と自信をもって見守っています。そして子ども達も本当にそれぞれの遊びを思うままにしているので、競った数値で測ったりできないけれど、確実に「身のこなし」がいろいろ変化してきています。木登りや土砂を削るなどいろんな動きを教えてもらうのではなく、子ども達が自身で経験し、獲得していくことが必要だと思います。

この園庭で大事にしたいのは「子どもの中から生まれてくる遊び」。そしてここは湧水が湧き出る町で、園庭の「さくらじま」もてっぺんから水が湧き出ます。だから円乗寺の園庭は「水と遊びの湧き出る園庭」。これからも子ども達からワクワクする遊びがどんどん生まれてくる場所にし続けたいと思っています。

今後の楽しみはブルーベリーやアーモンドの実り。さらにクヌギでどんぐり拾いなど想いは尽きません。

School and were impressed by their advanced equipment and planning. All these elements combined and expanded to create a playgarden where children can experience activities only possible during their childhood.

Sharing ideas about playgarden development from the viewpoint of childrearing and looking from the children's perspective, we designed a wonderfully irregular layout and discussed creating a biotope and a Kakiyama (persimmon hill) around a persimmon tree. Our dreams were nicely transformed into reality.

After the playgarden was completed, I told the teachers what Kawawa Nursery School Principal Terada had said: "If children can climb a hill, they can also climb down. We simply need to have confidence in their ability. If we help them too much, it slows them down. Small experiences build confidence and teach the children how to overcome challenges." Knowing that children are naturally fast learners gives us the confidence to trust in their ability. Children engage freely in a variety of activities every day, expanding their range as they develop. No one teaches them how to climb a tree or scoop sand, but they learn as they accumulate experience.

We want to focus on activities that children create by themselves. This school is located in a town with abundant spring water. The school, therefore, has a playgarden full of activities and water. We continue developing the playgarden with the children's enthusiasm and excitement about creating activities in mind.

We are also looking forward to harvesting blueberries and almonds. In autumn, we'll enjoy picking acorns. It is so exciting to think about the new activities that this playgarden allows children to experience.

円乗寺保育園の先生方：元々の園庭にはお寺でお迎えした鐘楼や、大きなモミジの木が子ども達を見守る／Teachers at Enjoji Nursery School: In the garden, a bell-tower and a large maple tree brought by the temple watch over children.

ふたつの水源が子ども達の遊びと心を潤す
―さくらじま―

Two water sources support activities that contribute to mental development
– Sakurajima –

暑い日は子ども達が次から次へと、噴き出す水に集まってくる／On hot days, children gather one after another to get splashed.

てっぺんから水飛沫を上げているのは「さくらじま」。鹿児島の保育園らしくネーミングされたカルデラ砂場は岩や木、そして水の要素も加わって、子ども達の遊びも十人十色。中には協力し合って、もっと楽しい遊びを創りあげています。その連係プレーはお見事です。

Sakurajima splashes water from its top.
The sand pool was named after Kagoshima's well-known volcano. With rocks, trees, and water, children can broaden their activities in many ways. They cooperate with one another to create fun activities. It is very nice to see their teamwork.

湧き出る水は思い通りにならないからこそ楽しい／It is more fun because the water splashes randomly.

―小さな勾玉デッキ＆ガチャポンプ―
– Small Jewel Deck & Gacha Pump –

夏は冷たく、冬は温かい井戸水。夏はスイカを冷やしてみたい／The well water is cool in summer, and warm in winter. It's fun to cool watermelons with the water in summer.

　泥んこで思う存分、遊んだ子はここで綺麗になってお部屋へ戻ります。ポンプの水は湧水町の井戸水。そしてお寺の隅にいた五右衛門風呂を活用した桶は、お泊り保育で露天風呂になりました。

After playing in the mud, children clean up here before going back into the classrooms. Water flowing from the pump is well water from the town. An old bathtub heated directly from beneath was made into an outdoor bath for the annual sleepover at the school.

お寺で出番を待ってた？／Was the tub waiting for this opportunity at the temple?

みんなでお風呂は楽しい／It's fun to take a bath.

【第1章】園庭を創造する

081

小さい子達の安心スペース ―縁側デッキとエントランススロープ―
A secure space for small children – Deck & Entrance Slope –

　園舎から直接、出られるデッキから、大きい子が縦横無尽に遊ぶ姿を最初はおとなしく見ていた小さい子達。小さくても「やりたい気持ち」は一緒。しばらくすると、すべり台を滑ったり、登ったり。どんなに小さくても遊びは一人前です。

Small children on the deck directly connected to the room were watching older children actively playing on the playgarden. Soon they started moving around by themselves, climbing up and sliding down the slide. Children are all the same and good at playing at any age.

左・右／小さい子達のリラックスした笑顔と果敢な挑戦が見られる場所／(Left & Right) A place where we can see smiles on the faces of relaxed children and watch their eager enthusiasm.

楽しさ湧き出る子どもの王国
Children's Kingdom full of enjoyment

【第1章】園庭を創造する

園歌の中にも双子のもみの木／Twin fir trees in the school song.

お寺のもみの木 三代通う
お隣の圓乗寺の境内は昔の園庭。100年以上前から子ども達が遊ぶ姿を見守ってきた双子のもみの木は、祖父母の代から親しまれてきたシンボルです。

Fir trees at the temple
Three generations have gone to the school. The precincts of Enjoji Temple were the nursery school's former playgarden. These twin fir trees have watched over children over 100 years. Symbols of the nursery school, they have been around for three generations.

⑥ 小さな勾玉デッキ／Small Jewel Deck

整地前の園庭／The land before the playgarden was built

083

①さくらじま／Sakurajima

不要になった石垣を再利用し、木と砂と石で造られた「さくらじま」。攻略するためにはさまざまな動きを身につける必要があります。

Sakurajima was made of recycled stonewalls, wood, sand, and stones. Children master a wide variety of movements to complete the stages.

いろんなところから湧き出る水。誰が一番うまく集められるかな？／
Water splashing from everywhere. Who is the best at collecting water?

②ブランコ／Swing

③ポンプ、砂場／Pump, Sand Pool

砂場に直接流れ込む水は
子ども達の想像力をさらに高めていきます。

The water flowing into the sand pool sparks the children's imagination.

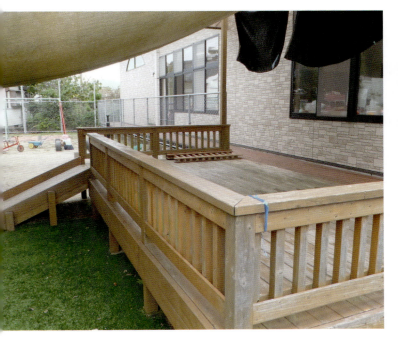

④縁側デッキ／Deck

シェードが日差しから守ってくれるデッキは
小さい子達の初めてがつまっている場所です。

The deck covered with shade is a place where small children have lots of first-time experiences.

⑤かきやま／Kakiyama (Persimmon Hill)

カキの実を目指して次から次へと木に登る子ども達。
そのカキの実も次の遊びへと大切に手渡されていきます。

Children climb the tree one after another to pick persimmons.
The persimmons they pick are used for the next activity.

男の子も女の子も、木に登る姿はそれぞれ／Both boys and girls climb the trees in their own way.

⑥ 小さな勾玉デッキ／Small Jewel Deck

パーゴラに茂るフジの涼しげな陰に
遊び疲れた子ども達がくつろぎに来ます。

When tired after playing, children come to the deck with its wisteria-covered pergola to relax in the shade.

小立野善隣館こども園 石川県金沢市
Kodatsuno Zenrinkan Kodomoen [Kanazawa City, Ishikara Prefecture]

土や水、樹木や花の香、陽の光の中で「生きる喜び」を実感できる遊び場

園長　吉田敬子先生

　当園は2006年より「子どもの運動能力を高める保育実践」の公開保育を行ったことがきっかけで、子どもの運動遊びと環境について考えるようになったのですが、最初は園内での運動遊びが中心で、「今日は〇〇の運動遊びをしましょう」と一斉に同じ遊びをさせて、保育士主導の保育になってしまうことが多かったんです。そこで2011年からは子どもの主体性を尊重し「好きな遊びが好きなだけ」できて、遊びを通して運動能力が身につくように、遊びに必要な環境についてアネビーさんと一緒に

A playgarden where children feel the pleasure of being surrounded by soil, water, trees, flowers, and sunshine

Keiko Yoshida, Principal

Since 2006, Kodatsuno Zenrinkan Kodomoen has demonstrated child rearing practices designed to improve physical capability, and this gave us a chance to consider the relationship between physical activity and the environment. At first, teachers tended to take the initiative in children's activities, which were mainly

考え、自然の中で四季の変化に気づいたり、見たりふれたりして遊べるように、さまざまな種類の樹木も植えてこの園庭づくりを始めました。

　最初は園庭の真ん中の築山。そしてその周りに土や水で十分に遊べる池を造り、土を盛ったんです。すると「泥んこ遊び」の経験のない若い保育士が子どもと一緒にどろどろになって遊ぶ姿や、満面の笑顔で歓声をあげ、心が満足していく子ども達を見ていると「遊び」について多岐にわたる環境が必要なのだと考えさせられました。

　また園庭では1歳から6歳までの異年齢の子ども達が好きな場所で同時に遊んでいて、大型遊具で遊ぶ大きい子を見て、小さい子が同じ事をしたくて挑戦するんですが、できた時はうれしくて何回でも、毎日でもやっています。

　子ども達はいろんな遊具やさまざまな場所で、時にはハラハラ、ドキドキしながら遊び、敏捷性、機敏性、判断力、人とのかかわり方を身につけていくんですね。子どもが自分から「やってみたい」と思ったことは、どの子もすごい自分の力を出しきって、果敢に挑戦していて、その姿を見ると本当に感動させられます。

　安全については危ないことを「させない」のではなく、遊びを通して危険を察知したり、回避したりして身を守る術を学び、経験として身につけながら子どもは育つのだと思っています。

　今日の園庭でも、子ども達の「生きる喜び」に満ちたドラマがいっぱい生まれています。

outdoor exercises for all children at the same time. From 2011, we considered ways to prioritize the independence of individual children and encourage them to develop their physical abilities through activities. We consulted with ANEBY staff to design the best environment for children, a playgarden where children can feel and touch seasonal changes in the wide variety of trees to be planted there.

We started from the hill at the center of the playgarden. Then we made a pond around the hill to provide children a place to play with soil and water. Young teachers were excited to play with the children, and the children had big smiles on their faces. Children thrive in an environment in which they can experience a wide range of activities.

Children at different ages play in different areas of the playgarden. Smaller children see older children playing on the larger equipment and try to do the same things. When they finally succeed in mastering an activity, they repeat it again and again every day.

Children play with different equipment at different places, experiencing the thrill of developing their agility, their judgment and the ability to build relationships with others. When they really want to do something, they utilize their entire ability to achieve the goal. I am so moved to see their growth.

We should give the children the freedom to explore and test their limits. Children instinctively know those limits, and activities allow them to expand those limits in a safe and secure environment.

Every day, stories of children filled with the pleasure of life are being written.

【第1章】園庭を創造する

小立野善隣館こども園の先生方：大型の遊具からの降り方を模索している子どもを、2時間以上も見守る先生も／Teachers at Kodatsuno Zenrinkan Kodomoen: Some teachers watch over children who have spent more than two hours exploring ways to come down from a large piece of playgarden equipment.

挑戦と達成の源　—2つの築山と3つのタワー—
Sources of Challenge and Achievement – Two Hills and Three Towers –

園庭の中央で小立野を象徴する築山は、鬼瓦の門をもち、子ども達の守り神のような存在／The hill in the center of the playgarden is a symbol of Kodatsuno. The small gate made of ridge-end tiles is like a guardian watching over the children.

ここからは自分たちの遊びの世界が一望できる／Children can see the entire playgarden and the activities taking place on it.

たくさんの仕掛けが待っているタワーは、子ども目線で見るとさらに心踊る／The tower has many surprises, and is a big thrill for the children.

登ったり、移動する手段はさまざま。挑戦は無限大／Different ways of moving. Children experiment to find ways.

　園庭を見渡す大きな築山と降雪などの天候にも左右されない人工芝の築山。子ども達は登ったり降りたりを自由自在にしながら、またてっぺんから次に遊ぶ場所を模索しながら、その登り降りさえも楽しんでいます。

　園庭を象徴する3つのタワーは互いに行き来することも挑戦であり、到着した先にはトランポリンや司令室、そして秘密の隠れ部屋があって、その先には空中ケーブルが。子ども達は次から次へと、そして毎日毎日難関と格闘し、誇らしい顔で達成していきます。

There is a large hill overlooking the entire playgarden, and a small hill covered with artificial grass that the children can play on rain or shine. Children climb up and down the hill, looking for places to explore next. Climbing up and down the playgarden's three symbolic towers is also a challenge for the children. After reaching the goal, a trampoline, a command center, and a hidden chamber await them. Ahead is the aerial cable. Children try hard to accomplish increasingly more challenging stages to achieve their goals.

実りの喜び、自然とのかかわり ―収穫と食育―
Pleasure of Harvest and Involvement with Nature – Harvesting and Food Education –

トンボがとまっているのは高い木の枝。めいっぱい背伸びしたらいっぱい捕まえられたね／Dragonflies land on the branches of a tall tree. Stretch your body and catch a lot.

大きい子は自分たちなりの足場を作って、ブドウ棚から美味しそうな実を収穫する／Older children make their own platforms to stand on to harvest delicious grapes from the trellis.

ここにはなんとピザ釜がある。調理室で用意した生地に、子ども達が収穫したピーマンやじゃがいもをのせて焼くとピーマンが甘いと大好評。またみんなで一緒に食べることがどんなことよりも、嬉しくて楽しい／This playgarden has a pizza oven. They often bake pizzas with the bell peppers and potatoes harvested by children. Children love the sweet bell peppers. Eating delicious pizzas together is a fun and enjoyable experience for them.

遊びも挑戦も十人十色
Different ways of playing and achieving goals

092

① **3つのタワー**／Three Towers

タワーへ登るのも、降りるのも、それぞれのタワーへの行き来も、すべてが新しい身のこなしを経験できるように造られています。そして各タワーのてっぺんには、ご褒美の遊びが待っています。

While climbing up and down the towers and down, and moving to different towers, children experience different ways of moving their bodies. After reaching the top of each tower, a fun activity awaits them.

てっぺん制覇のご褒美のひとつは「司令室」。座った子どもの顔はとても誇らしげ／The command center is one of the rewards that awaits children reaching the top of the towers. They look very proud.

② 空中ケーブル／Aerial Cable

タワーから伸びる空中ケーブルは勇者の証。そして次の勇者のためにシートを手渡しするのも勇者の仕事です。

Riding on the Aerial Cable from the tower is proof of confidence. Passing the sheet to the next brave child also builds confidence.

③ ピザ釜／Pizza Oven

④ じゃぶじゃぶ池／Jabu Jabu Pond

大きな石が使われていて、自然の渓流を想像させる。見学者に危なくないのかと聞かれることもしばしば。でも子ども達は事も無げに登ったり降りたりしています。

Large rocks are placed in the pond, reminding us of a natural mountain stream. Visitors often ask us if it is dangerous for children. But children climb up and down the rocks without a care.

⑤ 築山／Hill

この人工芝の築山は小さい子のお気に入り。思い思いの楽しみ方がある／Small children love this small hill covered with artificial grass. They enjoy their own activities here.

⑥ 築山／Hill

⑦ 小屋／Hut

全身を使って屋根登り。2歳児が挑戦することも／Climb up the roof using their entire body. Two-year-old children also try.

⑧ 砂場／Sand Pool

サラサラを楽しんだり、水を使って固めてみたり、全身を使って掘ってみたり、収穫したブドウで創作ケーキまでつくります。

Children enjoy dry sand, making it hard with water, and digging with their entire body. They make mud pies with grapes that they harvested.

【第1章】園庭を創造する

097

遊び場をつくる人たち －園庭デザイン研究所－

Specialists Engaged in Playgarden Development – Playgarden Design Institute –

大切にしていること

　アネビーの遊具は子ども達の遊びの段階によって難易度や規模を、積み木のように変化させることができるという特長をもっています。さらにその遊びが広がるような動線、そして自然遊びや植栽にまで、あらゆる「遊び」の可能性を探り、実現できるよう努めています。もちろん子ども達が遊んでいる時の「見守りやすさ」も重要です。また園がある場所は基本的に住宅地に在ることが多く、周囲の環境と調和し、受け入れられるかも考慮しています。だから工事中に近隣の方から「楽しみにしているよ」と声をかけていただくこともあり、嬉しく思っています。

設計×子ども

　遊具は子ども達にとってただの遊び道具ではなく、子ども達の世界を形づくる「家」なのだと私たちは考えています。だから決して「子ども騙し」にならないよう、子ども達の「やりたい」に真剣に応えられて、憧れを抱く遊び場であることを目指しています。そのために子ども達の「やりたい」と、先生方の「やらせたい」という夢をとことん語っていただくことも稀ではありません。その上で地域の風土や文化的背景の要素を取り入れたり、既存のものもうまく融合させたりして園独自の新しい世界観も同時に提案できるようにしています。もちろん予算という壁にぶつかることもありますが(笑)。でも先生方と本気で考え、一緒につくり上げた園庭だからこそ、私たちの想像を超えて遊びが広がっていく園庭になると信じています。

子ども達の愛する「遊び場」をつくりたい

　遊具は子ども達にとっての大切な「家」。だから思い入れもたくさんあります。新たに園庭をつくる時には、以前からある遊具と「さよなら」しなくてはならないし、工事の間は遊具で遊ぶことができません。だから「こわさないで」とお願いされることも。でも新しい遊具が完成すると「つくってくれてありがとう」と喜ぶ顔とともに、歓声をあげて遊具の中を駆け回っている姿をみると充実感でいっぱいになります。ここだけの話ですが、ポストのある「家」には時々、子ども達宛に誰かからの手紙が届くそうですよ。

Our Priority

The level and scale of Aneby playgarden equipment can be rearranged like blocks according to the stage of activity. We consider the full range of activities, the flow of children's movement, the surrounding nature, and the greenery that expands growth. It is also important to consider the ease with which staff can monitor safety. Since nursery schools and kindergartens are often located in residential areas, we also consider harmony with the surrounding environment. People in the community often tell us, " We are looking forward to seeing the finished playgarden, " which makes us very happy.

Designing and Children

We consider playgarden equipment not simply as tools for play, but as a home that forms the children's world. Therefore, we strive to completely understand children's desires to develop playgardens that enable children to fulfill those desires. To ensure the success of the playgardens we design, we make teacher input a priority. After fully understanding the image and intent, we factor in elements such as the climate and cultural background of the community, and consider the integration of existing equipment to create the best proposal for each school. Of course, working within a school's budget is and should be an important consideration. We believe that it is important for us to discuss all aspects of playgarden design to ensure a proposal that maximizes the potential for children's activities.

We Create Playgardens that Children Love

Playgarden equipment leaves children with special feelings and lots of memories. When playgarden equipment is changed, the children say good-bye to the old equipment and will not be able to play during construction. Children often ask us not to take the old equipment away; but when they see the new equipment, they are very happy and excited as they run around the playgarden. It is at that moment that we feel the satisfaction of our work. Children sometimes receive letters in the mailbox installed in the equipment.

【第2章】
さまざまな園庭

[Chapter II]

The Variety of Playgarden Layouts

それぞれの広さ、それぞれの条件、それぞれの想い。
園庭という遊び環境をつくるためには、たくさんの乗り越えるべき目標があります。
ここで紹介するのは園の特色やこだわり、またその園で必要な遊びの要素、
そして地形や予算などの物理的な要素に鑑みて、提案してきた園庭です。
問題点が逆の発想につながり、できあがった遊具や、
園のシンボルツリーや既存の遊具を活かした園庭も次々に生まれています。
たくさんの子ども達の遊び場をご覧ください。

There are many elements to be considered when creating a playgarden that meets the kindergarten's expectations and is ideal for conditions.

In this chapter, we introduce some playgarden layouts that carefully consider the characteristics, focus and budget of individual schools as well as planned activities and physical elements such as ground features.

The problems we encountered led to innovative solutions.

We also made proposals that incorporated existing trees and playgarden equipment.

We hope you will enjoy our work.

園庭は里山

泥んこ遊びや水と戯れる楽しさ、木々や草花とともに感じる四季、自然と生きる子どもは想像力と慈しみにあふれています。

Our playgarden is a small world of nature
The fun of playing with soil and water surrounded by beautiful trees, plants and flowers throughout the year in this small world of nature fills the children with wonder and nurtures their imagination.

子ども達を包み込む フジ繁る都会の森
立正佼成会附属 佼成育子園　東京都杉並区

Urban forests filled with wisteria embrace the children
Rissho Koseikai Kosei Ikujien/ Suginami-ku, Tokyo

どんな遊具でも子ども達は自分なりの遊び方を見つけ、やる気と笑顔で満ちている／
The equipment and layout encourage the children to discover their own positive ways of playing.

木や土の色と調和するこだわった素材でつくられた園庭は、子ども達が「やりたい」と思うことがすべてつめ込まれた都会の森になりました。園庭を滑走する空中ケーブルや綱渡りのようにドキドキするV字ブリッジも、動きの楽しさを知るゆりかごやトランポリンも、創意工夫でいろんな遊びができる築山や砂場も、そして園庭中に育つフジやたくさんの植物も。この園庭に在るものは、すべてが子ども達の好奇心を満たす遊びの要素です。

Harmonizing playgarden equipment with the colors of trees and soil creates an exciting urban forest with many plants and flowers. It features items such as an aerial cable that sparks curiosity, a thrilling V-shape bridge that feels like a tightrope, a cradle and trampoline that let the children enjoy the thrill of motion, and a hill and sand pool that encourage children to exercise their imaginations for various activities.

小さな小さな築山は、小さな子どもの冒険の山／
A tiny hill is a mountain adventure for small children.

以前の園庭／Previous playgarden

現在の園庭／Current playgarden

設置内容
築山／Ｖ字ブリッジ／デッキ／ゆり
かごスウィング／プレイターフ　ほか

Installed Equipment
Hill/ V-shape Bridge/ Deck/
Cradle Swing/ Play Turf, etc.

伝統を受け継ぎ
感性豊かな大人に育て！
嵯峨幼稚園　京都府京都市

Nurturing sensitivity and tradition
Saga Kindergarten/ Kyoto City, Kyoto Prefecture

足元の安定しないＶ字ブリッジの上を歩くのは足元の景色も見えてスリリング／It's very thrilling to walk on the V-shape bridge while looking down.

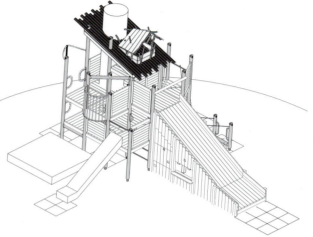

設置内容
HAGSユニプレイ・オリジナル複合遊具／園庭劇場／築山／ガチャポンプ／空中ケーブル　ほか

Installed Equipment
HAGS Uniplay & Original Compound Playgarden Equipment/ Playgarden Theater/ Hill/ Gacha Pump/ Aerial Cable, etc.

あらかしやぐら：京都の町家でよく見る「通り庭」を遊びの空間に。和紙の照明があるロフトや、日差しが漏れる格子扉が「和」の心を育てます／Quercus Glauca Turret: We have made a garden passage (tori-niwa) that evokes those seen in townhouses in Kyoto into a fun space. The loft with lighting from Japanese paper and lattice doors filled with sunshine nurture the spirit of Japanese tradition.

挑戦とくつろぎ／Challenging and Comfortable

カニカニ横丁／Crab Walking Path (Kani Kani Yokocho)

樹齢200年以上のアラカシを「じぞう池」が囲み、その水流れには旧園舎の瓦が「龍背城」を形づくり、そして梁が「築山」のひょうたんトンネルを支えています。園の長い歴史を刻んできたそれらは、これからも子ども達の育みを見守って、「子ども達の外遊びをもっと充実させたい」という園長先生の想いと共に、また新しい時間を育てています。最近では京文化への慈しみを学べる遊び空間が増え、子ども達は挑戦を続けています。

The pond was built around a large quercus glauca tree believed to be more than 200 years old. The water flows into a pond made using roof tiles from the former kindergarten building, and old beams support the tunnel running through the hill. These have been at the heart of the kindergarten, watching the children grow over time, as an expression of the Principal's desire to create meaningful outdoor activities that promote healthy development. The kindergarten also provides the children with their first encounter with the culture of Kyoto, and encourages them to continue learning.

大きな木々と融合した「天空散歩(そらんぽ)」は子どもの成長を願う場所
誠心相陽幼稚園　神奈川県相模原市

A walk in the sky (*Soranpo*) integrated with large trees – A wonderful place that promotes growth
Seishin Soyo Kindergarten/ Sagamihara City, Kanagawa Prefecture

地球上で一番古い植物メタセコイアも、サクラとともに子ども達の大きな成長を願っている／Metasequoia, the oldest tree on the earth, watches the children grow along with cherry trees.

秋の醍醐味、デッキのくぼみに落ち葉のプール／Autumn charm – A pool of fallen leaves in a pit on the deck.

敷地内の森にはネットの海がたくさん張り巡らされており、「揺れる」感覚を楽しんでいる／The children enjoy swinging on the net seas placed among the forests throughout the playgarden.

【第2章】さまざまな園庭

　大きなサクラの樹の下に園のみんなで「天空散歩（そらんぽ）」と名付けた遊具が、子ども達の訪れを待っています。挑戦する要素がたくさんつまった遊具を登り切った上からの眺めは最高です。友達との交流や楽しい自然遊びのできる、心も体も憩うこもれびデッキも人気の遊び場です。先生方は遊具への理解を深め、子ども達自身の力を信じて「やりたい」気持ちを大切に、そして子ども達と同じくらい元気に接しています。

A piece of playgarden equipment that everyone at the kindergarten calls *Soranpo* (skywalk) awaits children under a large cherry tree. The view from the top of the equipment is fantastic, and the children enjoy the challenges that the climb presents. The Sunshine Deck is very popular with the children as a place where they can interact with one another and have fun playing comfortably in a natural setting. Teachers understand of the equipment's functions, trust the children's ability and potential to grow, and play enthusiastically with them.

見守りポイント例／Example of Supervising Spot

平面図／ground plan

設置内容
オリジナル複合遊具／築山／ネットの海

Installed Equipment
Original Compound Playgarden Equipment/ Hill/ Net Sea

107

シンボルタワーHAGS

HAGSの遊具は園や地域のランドマークタワーとなり、子ども達の憧れ、そして成長のシンボルになります。

HAGS Equipment
The entire set of HAGS playgarden equipment serves as a landmark in the kindergarten and the community. They are symbolic of the children's growth.

フジ棚のお城は憧れと挑戦のシンボル
住の江幼稚園　大阪府大阪市

The castle covered with wisteria is a symbol of wonder and the spirit of challenge
Suminoe Kindergarten/ Osaka City, Osaka Prefecture

【第2章】さまざまな園庭

フジ棚と融合したネットトンネルは、下が見えてスリリング／The net tunnel integrated with wisteria trellises offers a thrilling view of the ground below.

109

「こどもの砦塔」は地域のランドマークタワーとなっていて屋根の頂上は11mを超える。頑張って登った景色も特別な景色／The Children's Fortress and Turret exceeds 11 meters at the top of the roof, and has become a landmark in the community. The view from the top is very special.

　夢中になれる楽しさがあること、そして運動を通じて脳神経の発達を促す構造であることを両方満たす挑戦する遊具として、「こどもの櫓砦」と名付けられたこの遊具はたくさんの試行錯誤とともに生まれました。「年長児の身体能力が無ければ登れず、それを眺める年少・年中児が"早く登れるようになりたい"と憧れを抱くような遊具にしたかった」という園長先生の願い。今、砦は子ども達を夢中にし、攻略した時の達成感と喜びで満ちあふれています。

The equipment was named Children's Fortress and Turret (*Kodomo no Yagura*). It provides children the opportunity to focus on fun and has a structure that promotes the development of the cranial nerves. The equipment was developed through trial and error. The Principal wanted to install playgarden equipment that older children could climb as younger children watched on with the desire to try to be like them. This equipment has captured the hearts of children and filled them with happiness and a feeling of accomplishment.

この砦はフジ棚を中心に大きな空間を回遊性と複雑な階層をもつ構造となっており、子ども達は自然の中で遊んでいるように縦横無尽に行きかっている。塔のてっぺんにある高さ5mを超えるチューブスライドから降りてくる顔は誇らしさと笑顔でいっぱい／This equipment allows a large space around a wisteria trellis with a complex layered structure where children can move about freely as if they were playing in nature. Children enjoy the tube slide running from the top of the tower more than 5 meters high. They have smiles on their faces and pride in their hearts.

設置内容
HAGSユニプレイ・オリジナル複合遊具

Installed Equipment
HAGS Uniplay & Original Compound Playgarden Equipment

【第2章】さまざまな園庭

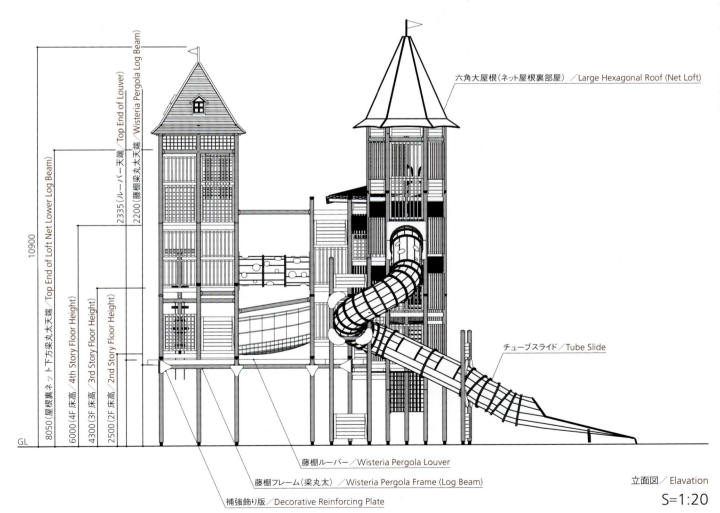

立面図／Elavation
S=1:20

遊具は園のシンボルだけじゃない
楽しく遊んで体力・我慢・限界を学ぶ

松本幼稚園　東京都江戸川区

Playgarden equipment is not only a symbol of the kindergarten, but also an important way to develop physical strength and endurance while teaching limits.

Matsumoto Kindergarten/ Edogawa-ku, Tokyo

遊具とその周辺は毎朝、先生方が30分ほどかけて綺麗に清掃するため、遊具の床はいつもピカピカ。裸足で遊ぶ子ども達は思う存分、遊びに集中できる／Teachers clean the playgarden equipment and the surrounding areas for 30 minutes every morning. The base of the equipment is always clean and shiny. Children in bare feet play to their heart's content.

設置内容
HAGSユニプレイ・オリジナル複合遊具／ゆりかごスウィング／プレイターフ／築山／鉄棒／ブランコ

Installed Equipment
HAGS Uniplay & Original Compound Playgarden Equipment/ Cradle Swing/ Play Turf/ Hill/ Bar/ Swing

園のそばを流れる川の遊歩道からも壮大な遊具が見える。地域の方にも注目の遊具／The large playgarden equipment can be seen from the walking path along the river that runs near the kindergarten.

　以前の遊具は大切にされ、取り壊しの時は惜しむ声も。そのため今回、遊具を設計するにあたって、同じアイテムを揃えながらもそれ以上の遊びができるように考えられました。HAGSの遊具はもちろん、芝に覆われた築山から既存の砂場まで、子ども達は時間いっぱい回遊して遊んでいます。「遊具はシンボルだけじゃない。遊んで楽しくて体力をつけることができて、我慢や限界を学び、遊び勝手が良いのが遊具」と園長先生。同じ遊具でも年齢ごとにいろんな遊び方ができるこの遊具に、今日も子ども達は真剣に取り組んでいます。

The old equipment had been used for a long period of time and some people wanted it to stay. Therefore, in designing the new equipment, they chose the same items as before but considered combinations that would provide greater chances for activities. In addition to HAGS equipment, hills covered with grass and existing sand pools provide children chances to play until the end of their play time. The Principal thinks of the playgarden equipment not as a symbol of the kindergarten, but as important tools that give children the chance to play, increase their physical strength and endurance, and learn limits. Children can create different activities according to their age.

立面図／Elavation
S=1:200

予期せぬことが起こる自然
その体験で自らを育てる園庭

明彩幼稚園　埼玉県新座市

Nature where the unexpected occurs
Playgarden where every child develops ability through experience

Meisai Kindergarten/ Niiza City, Saitama Prefecture

全体イメージパース／Complete Perspective Drawing

遊びがいっぱい。そしてまだまだ発展途上／
Plenty of activities and still developing

設置内容
HAGSユニプレイ・オリジナル複合遊具／砂場＆ガチャポンプ／パーゴラ／築山／こもれびデッキ　ほか

Installed Equipment
HAGS Uniplay & Original Compound Playgarden Equipment/ Sand Pool & Gacha Pump/ Pergola/ Hill/ Sunshine Deck, etc.

　「何十年ぶりに秘密基地をつくっている時のようにワクワクした」とおっしゃるのは子ども達と一緒に泥んこ遊びをしている園長先生。園で子ども達が予期せぬことがおきる自然を感じ、自由に群れて遊べる体験を毎日できないかと考え、「からだ遊びの場所」にするべく、この園庭をつくりました。例えば「転んだら痛い」という感覚は転んでこそ理解できるし、けがをしないように手で支える動きを自ら体験することで、子ども達の経験値が伸びていくためです。さらに子ども達は「遊び」を通してルールを守ることや、同じ年齢の友達同士だけでなく、年長の子が年少の子に対してお互いに思いやることを自然にできるようになっています。先生方も「見守る」姿勢を大切にしているため、今日も子ども達は自ら遊び、自ら育っていきます。

The Principal said, as he played in the mud with the children, "It is as fun as it was when I was a youngster making a secret base with my friends." He believes that it is important to provide children with a place to play as freely as they wish surrounded by nature and which something unexpected always happens. With that belief, he planned this playgarden. For example, children learn through experience that it is painful when they fall, and this helps them learn to support their body to prevent injuries. They also learn naturally how to follow rules and learn to be considerate of others, not only their friends, but also smaller children. Teachers prioritize watching over children as they play to help them grow mentally and physically.

挑戦も回遊する
庭いっぱいに、また高低差を利用して、
多様な動きと挑戦意欲が連続した遊びにつながります。

Challenges await the children
The differences in the level of the playgarden surface give the children the opportunity to make a wide variety of movements which lead to development.

自由な遊びが生み出す
自己管理とリスク回避の学び
山梨学院小学校　山梨県甲府市

Lesson for self-management and risk prevention developed through free activities
Yamanashi Gakuin Elementary School/ Kofu City, Yamanashi Prefecture

[第2章] さまざまな園庭

理想の教育環境をもとめて、子どもの「自由」が もっとも引き出される運動器具

校長　山内紀幸 博士（教育学）

　本校にはチャイムも教室の壁もありませんが、子ども達は始業時間には自分の席で集中しています。また遊具にも細かな規則はありませんが、異学年が混在しても毎日賑やかに遊んでいます。なぜでしょうか？　それは選択や工夫を認める「自由」の保証と、行動結果に対しての「責任」の自覚があるからです。子ども達はどうすれば最大限に学べるかを本能的に知っています。自分の限界を見極めつつ果敢に挑戦し、相手の行動にも気を配り、トラブル回避のための自己管理の術を学び、心も育てています。

　スウェーデンのHAGS社の遊具はヨーロッパの安全基準をクリアし、デザイン性にも優れ、小学生向けにカスタマイズできる子どもの「自由」をもっとも引き出せる運動器具だと思います。高さ3m近くある登り棒や2階デッキからのチューブスライドなど、一見すると危険に思える「リスク」こそが大型遊具の魅力です。「できるかもしれない」という適度な負荷が無いと子どもの挑戦は生まれず、「ヒヤッ」とする感覚を味わってこそ、危険回避のための身のこなし方が学習できます。「リスク」を全部排除してしまえば、怪我はゼロになるかもしれませんが、大切なことを学ばずに終わってしまうかもしれません。「リスク」は学びの重要なスパイスです。

　しかし「ハザード（重大事故）」に至ることが無いよう、落下吸収マットを敷設し、定期点検と教員による日々の点検も実施しています。また使用時には、必ず大人の目で見守っています。

Seeking a desirable educational environment – Playgarden equipment that allows children to exert their freedom to the greatest degree

Principal: PhD. Noriyuki Yamauchi (Pedagogy)

This elementary school does not have chimes to signal classes, or walls between rooms. However, children sit in their seats and prepare for class. There are no hard and fast rules about playgarden equipment, and children at different ages play together without problems. Why? It is because we guarantee freedom of choice, and they are aware of their responsibility for their actions. Children know instinctually how to maximize their learning. They feel their limits, boldly take on challenges, consider the behaviors of others, learn how to prevent troubles, and learn self-management.

The playgarden equipment from HAGS in Sweden meets European safety standards, has excellent designability, and can be customized freely for elementary school students. The climbing bar, which is 3 meters tall, and the tube slide connected to the second-floor deck may look dangerous at first glance, but they are the attraction of large-scale equipment. The equipment provides the appropriate degree of difficulty, enough that the children feel challenged but not so much that it stifles their motivation to try. When they feel a degree of trepidation, they come to learn how to anticipate risks. If we eliminate all the risks for children, they may not be injured; but then they cannot learn to protect themselves. Risk is an important experience for learning.

However, it is also important for us to prevent serious accidents. We have placed mats on the ground to absorb impact, and teachers conduct daily inspections. While children are using the equipment, we always watch over them.

イメージパース／Perspective Drawing

設置内容
HAGSユニプレイ・オリジナル複合遊具

Installed Equipment
HAGS Uniplay & Original Compound Playgarden Equipment

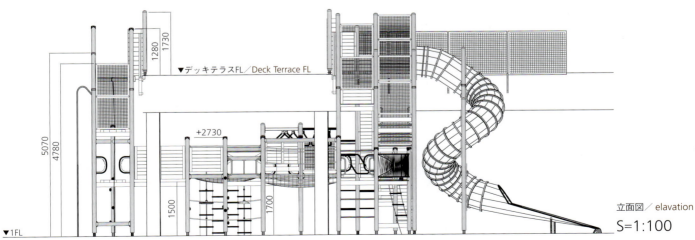

立面図／elavation
S=1:100

【第2章】さまざまな園庭

ラージヒルのてっぺんにはご褒美も／There is a reward at the top of the large hill.

校庭を見下ろすラージヒル
そこは未知の動きと挑戦力を満たす場所

昭和女子大学附属 昭和小学校　東京都世田谷区

A large hill looking down on the playground where children try new movements and nurture their desire to take on challenges

Showa Women's University Showa Elementary School/ Setagaya-ku, Tokyo

てっぺんのご褒美は天井に映し出される空、「動く絵画」／
The reward for children who reach the top is a beautiful sky.

上／のぼってるの？ おりてるの？ 下／上からの眺めは爽快／
(Above) Are you climbing up or down? (Below) A fantastic view from the top

　広い校庭の奥、そこには子ども達の征服欲をくすぐるラージヒルがそびえ、その周りにはあらゆる未知の動きを体の隅々まで体験できる大きな遊び場があります。そこで日々、子ども達は新しい遊びと楽しみを見つけ出すことに真剣。その遊びの空間は、一人ひとりの子が限界を見据えることなく、ひたすら挑戦力を満たすことに一生懸命になれる場所。登ったり、降りたり、つかまったり、背伸びしたり、かがんだり。「動き」でいっぱいになったら、今度はゆらゆら揺れたり、座ったり、時には空を覗いてみる。すると「心」もいっぱいになって、「生きるための基礎経験」を育てた子どもがたくさん生まれています。

Deep in the expansive area is a large hill surrounded by a large playground where all sorts of new movement can be experienced. Children eagerly explore new activities and fun every day. The space helps children attempt new challenges without feeling individual limits. They climb up and down, hold onto things, stretch, bend, and more. After moving a lot, the children can swing, sit, and look up at the sky. They end up mentally and physically satisfied. The children enrolled in this school grow through these important experiences.

設置内容
HAGSユニプレイ・オリジナル複合遊具／フリーフォールネット／まがたまデッキ／クライミング／バランスロープ ほか

Installed Equipment
HAGS Uniplay & Original Compound Playgarden Equipment/ Free Fall Net/ Jewel Deck/ Climbing Wall/ Balance Rope, etc.

自然の森に負けない園庭で挑戦意欲を大きく育てる
おおぞらひまわり保育園　神奈川県横浜市

「どんぐりこどもとりで」は上に登るための階段はありません。でもうんていやファイヤーマンポール、ネット、ロープ、クライミング等、たくさんの登り口を利用して子ども達は果敢にてっぺんへ。「園庭は心の開放の場」という園長先生のお考え通り、子ども達は野山で遊びまわっていた昔の子どものように、遊びという自由を満喫しています。

Helping children to enjoy challenges in a playgarden surrounded by nature
Ozora Himawari Nursery School/ Yokohama City, Kanagawa Prefecture

Acorn Fortress for Children (*Donguri Kodomo Toride*) does not have stairs. It has overhead ladders, fireman poles, nets, ropes, and climbing walls that provide ways to the top. The principal believes that playgardens are a place for children to develop their minds, and the children here fully enjoy activities like those of olden days, running through the hills and mountains.

左／以前の園庭。右／遊具は一番奥へ／(Left) Previous playgarden (Right) The equipment is installed at the far end of the playgarden.

斜面の園庭に、泥や水とふれ合う自然の森のような環境づくりから始め、さらに遊び込むためラージヒルのある「とりで」をつくった／
Starting from the creation of an environment like a natural forest with mud and water on the slope, a fortress with a large hill was developed.

築山／Hill

ガチャポンプ&水流れ／Gacha Pump & Water Flow

設置内容
HAGSユニプレイ・オリジナル複合遊具／築山／井戸&ガチャポンプ／プレイビオトープ　ほか

Installed Equipment
HAGS Uniplay & Original Compound Playgarden Equipment/ Hill/ Well & Gacha Pump/ Biotope, etc.

憩いと挑戦

元気に走り回って挑戦したい時、何かを作りたいと一心不乱な時、友達とかかわりたい時。それぞれの場所で思う存分。

Comfortable and challenging

When they want to run around and try something new, when they concentrate on making things, when they want to play with friends. All children enjoy playing to their heart's desire at different places.

自然も遊びも満喫
オープンカフェのある園庭
認定こども園 かほる保育園　山梨県甲府市

Enjoy activities in nature
A playgarden with an open café deck
Certified Center for Early Childhood Education, Kahoru Nursery School/
Kofu City, Yamanashi Prefecture

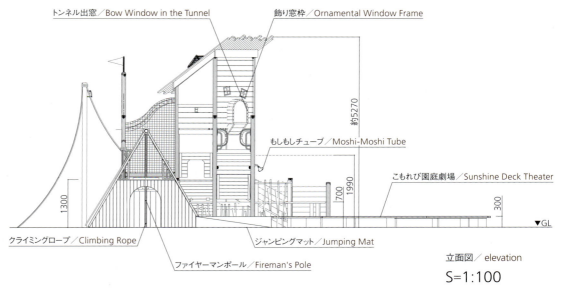

トンネル出窓／Bow Window in the Tunnel	飾り窓枠／Ornamental Window Frame
もしもしチューブ／Moshi-Moshi Tube	こもれび園庭劇場／Sunshine Deck Theater
クライミングロープ／Climbing Rope	ジャンピングマット／Jumping Mat
ファイヤーマンポール／Fireman's Pole	

立面図／elevation　S=1:100

　この園庭は最初にできた築山を中心に、水遊びや泥んこ遊び、そしてたくさんの植物がある自然遊びの場所と、サクラとフジの咲く癒しのデッキと、子ども達の挑戦の場である遊具の場所のふたつの特徴をもっています。

　フジの花の香りが漂うデッキはグリーンの日よけが心地良く、子ども達はのびのびと過ごし、時にはオープンカフェのようにみんなでお弁当を広げる光景が見られます。

　もちもちの木の枝を足掛かりに登れば、てっぺんには達成者だけが鳴らせるマリーンベルが。さらに複雑な階層をもつ遊具がさらなる子ども達の挑戦を待っています。

The playgarden at this school has a hill surrounded by areas where children can play with water, mud, and plants to achieve something new every day. It is also equipped with a comfortable deck where cherry blossoms and wisteria bloom beautifully in season.

The deck with the scent of wisteria floating over it is comfortable under the shade of greens. The children relax here and can eat lunch as if it were an open café.

After climbing up the *Courage Tree* (*Mochimochi no Ki*) using the branches, a marine bell is waiting at the top for those that make the climb. There is also another piece of equipment with complex layers waiting for children to conquer.

【第2章】さまざまな園庭

以前の園庭／Previous playgarden

設置内容
HAGSユニプレイ・オリジナル複合遊具／プレイターフ／デッキ　ほか

Installed Equipment
HAGS Uniplay & Original Compound Playgarden Equipment/ Play Turf/ Deck, etc.

陽だまりで遊ぶ子ども達は体も心も豊かに育つ
ひなもり保育園　宮崎県日南市

Children develop both mentally and physically through play-time activities in the sunshine
Hinamori Nursery School/ Nichinan City, Miyazaki Prefecture

　この園の子どもはすごく挑戦的で塔のてっぺんを制覇すべく、さまざまな登り口から次々と登って行きます。その二つの塔をつなぐのは下が見えるネットの橋だったり、降りるのも長いチューブスライドだったりと子ども達の「遊びたい」をたくさん満足させてくれます。その中でも子ども達が意欲的に挑戦するのはマットへのジャンプ。真剣な顔で果敢に挑戦し、着地に成功すると満面の笑顔に変わります。そんな陽だまりで思い思いに遊ぶ子ども達を、双頭の高い塔がそびえる遊具が今日も見守っています。

Children at this school are very active. They climb to the top of the towers from different starting points. The two towers are connected by a net bridge from which the children can see the ground, and they ride the long tube slide back down. These play-time activities are very popular. The children love to jump down onto the mats. They are absorbed by the thrill and smile happily after landing. These two towers are always watching over the children playing in the sunshine.

下が見えてスリリング／Thrilling to see below

憩いの場でゆっくりお話し／Chatting on the comfortable deck

陽だまりでくつろぐと気持ちいい／Feeling good relaxing on the deck

こんな高さもジャーンプ／Jumping from up high

【第2章】さまざまな園庭

設置内容
HAGSユニプレイ・オリジナル複合遊具／築山／パーゴラ／こもれびデッキ　ほか

Installed Equipment
HAGS Uniplay & Original Compound Playgarden Equipment/ Hill/ Pergola/ Sunshine Deck, etc.

立面図／elavation
S=1:100

築山を登ったり、降りたり。またポンプで水をくみ上げれば楽しいじゃぶじゃぶ池が出現。塀も木製のため圧迫感がなく、外の景色までも園庭の景色となり開放感にあふれている／Children climb up and down the hill. The Jabu Jabu Pond appears after pumping the water. Wooden fences blend with the natural atmosphere of the playgarden. Integrating the neighborhood buildings with the playgarden, it looks very open and wide.

美しく整えられた園庭で
子ども達は遊びつくす

片岡の里保育園　奈良県北葛城郡

Children enjoy playing at this beautiful playgarden
Kataoka no Sato Nursery School/ Kitakatsuragi-gun, Nara Prefecture

以前の園庭：水はけが悪く、外遊びに困ることがしばしば。そのため人工芝とマットを全面敷設した。今では子どもも思い切って走り回っている／Previous playgarden: The drainage was slow and children often could not play outside. Therefore, artificial turf and mats are installed over the entire playgarden. Children now enjoy running around every day.

設置内容
HAGSユニプレイ・オリジナル複合遊具／ユニミニ／築山／じゃぶじゃぶ池　ほか

Installed Equipment
HAGS Uniplay & Original Compound Playgarden Equipment/ UniMini/ Hill/ Jabu Jabu Pond, etc.

　森の中を駆け巡るように設計された園庭は、運動能力の低下を改善したいという想いからつくられました。そのためさまざまな動きに挑戦できる遊具と、子ども達が自発的に遊びを創造できる仕掛けをたくさん用意しました。

This playgarden was designed to allow children to run around between the trees to improve their physical ability. A wide variety of equipment and items were installed to accustom the children to various movements and encourage them to create activities.

園庭にはたくさんの種類の木々が植栽されている。これから10年後には「森の中の園庭」に／The playgarden has many trees. It will be like a playgarden in a forest in 10 years.

斜面も遊び場

斜面のある場所は子ども達が大好きで挑戦したいと思う場所。
その場所に期待以上の遊び場を与えます。

The slope is also a fun place to play
Children love to climb the slope.
We installed playgarden equipment on the slope to encourage them to explore new skills.

「冒険の丘」はスリル満点
大人の「難しい」は子どもの「やってみたい」
東たいてん保育園　東京都東村山市

The Adventure Hill is thrilling
Children are always eager to try new things
Higashi Taiten Nursery School/ Higashi-Murayama City, Tokyo

下から見上げても壮観。でも子ども達には挑戦意欲があふれる眺め／The view from below is also magnificent. This view also motivates children.

　この斜面を活かした園庭をつくりたいと思った園長先生に、最初は反対の意見もあったそうです。でも「芝すべり」をやらせたい、挑戦する心を養ってほしいと、この「冒険の丘」をつくりました。今では保護者の方々からも他の園からも、ぜひ遊ばせてほしいと言われるそうです。

　初めはルールも厳しく、先生方も慎重になっていたそうですが、子ども達の「やってみたい！」という気持ちがどんどん膨らんできてるのを感じて、徐々に自由度を上げていっているとのこと。だからできなかった子ができるようになって、何回も何回も挑戦する姿に先生方も一緒に喜んでいます。

Although the principal wanted to make a playgarden using the slope, some teachers were concerned. Finally they all agreed on having a slope as a slide to encourage children to slide down. Recently, parents and people from other kindergartens have wanted their children to play on the slope.

They started with strict rules for safety. However, as they saw the children's ability, they gradually loosened the rules to let them play within the range of ensured safety. Teachers are also happy to see the children who have tried and tried again finally succeed.

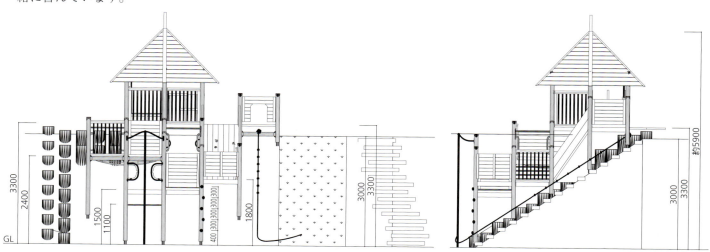

立面図（左／正面、右／右側面）／Elevation [(Left) Front Face, (Right) Right Side]　S=1:100

スリルをとことん楽しむ場所あり、想いを形にするところあり、すべてが子ども達にとって楽しい場所／This is the place to enjoy thrills and form motivation into action. The slope is fun for children.

設置内容
HAGSユニプレイ・オリジナル複合遊具／砂場＆ガチャポンプ＆ランダムフェンス　ほか

Installed Equipment
HAGS Uniplay & Original Compound Playgarden Equipment/ Sand Pool & Gacha Pump & Random Fence, etc.

園舎をはさんだ逆側の園庭には、園舎の側に砂場とガチャポンプ、そして奥には新しい挑戦の砦。これからこのふたつを繋いで園庭を囲むように、20mを超える挑戦の遊び場が広がっていく／On the other side of the school building, there is another playgarden with a sand pool, Gacha Pump, and new towers. Children expand their activities along with the flow of movement by connecting two playgardens that surround the entire school.

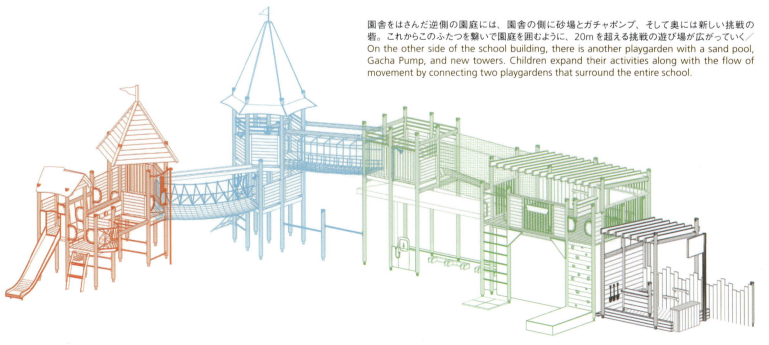

【第2章】さまざまな園庭

斜面をとことん遊ぶ子は
何度だって上へ登る楽しさを知っている
成田保育園　千葉県成田市

Children who climb up the slope know the excitement of reaching the top
Narita Nursery School/ Narita City, Chiba Prefecture

日当たりのいい斜面に大きく構えた遊具は横から見ても壮観。その姿は遠くに通る国道からも注目されているそう／The large equipment installed on the sunny slope is a splendid sight from the side as well. It can be seen from the national road that runs at some distance from the school.

男の子達がすべり台を3人で一緒に滑るのが流行り。我先にとすべり台へ殺到する／Their trend is for three boys to slide down together. They rush to the slide.

「さあ、いいよ」の掛け声とともに、園舎とつながる1階から子ども達が一斉に一番上まで登ってきます。手足を掛けて全身を使わないと到達できないてっぺんですが、その速さは3分もかかりません。登り切った子ども達は、誇らしげにトランポリンやすべり台を何度も何度も楽しんでいます。大きな遊具にもかかわらず斜面に設置したことで、もし落下しても地面が近くにあり、大きなけがにもつながりづらいとのこと。先生方も子ども達を見守りながら一緒に遊びを楽しむ事に積極的で、のんびりトランポリンに座っていた子ども達の真ん中にジャンプ。すると、反動で大きく飛び上がった子ども達は大喜びです。ここはそんな歓声が絶えない遊び場です。

"OK, it's ready" As soon as a teacher tells the children, they run from the 1st level connected to the school building to the top of the equipment. Although the children need to use their entire body to climb up to the top, it takes them only three minutes. After they reach the top, they try the trampoline and slide again and again. Placing this large equipment on the slope keeps it close to the ground, which prevents injury in case of falls. Teachers also enjoy playing while watching over the children, and sometimes jump into the middle of the children playing on the trampoline. The children are excited about being bounced up. This is such a fun place filled with shouts of joy.

設置内容
HAGSユニプレイ・オリジナル複合遊具／ユニミニ　ほか

Installed Equipment
HAGS Uniplay & Original Compound Playgarden Equipment/ UniMini, etc.

139

遊び場をつくる人たち －製造部－
Specialists Engaged in Playgarden Development – Manufacturing Department –

大切にしていること

製造する上で一番大切なのは子ども達が安心して遊ぶことができる遊具をつくることです。危険寸法に該当する箇所ができないようにし、ビスなど子ども達にケガをさせてしまうような部材忘れには細心の注意を払っています。鉄の切り子が出る作業の場合は、磁石を使って切り子が飛び散らないように工夫しています。

使っている工具も扱い方を間違えると危険なものもあるので、万が一、子どもが触ってケガをしてしまわないように、現場を離れる際は電動工具のコンセントを抜くといった対策を取っています。

製造×子ども

遊具が完成するまでに、先生方が子ども達にどんな説明をしているのかは園によって異なります。設計書を見ながら、先生が子ども達に対して「今ここをつくっているんだよ」と説明しながら一緒に完成を待ちわびている園もありますし、どんな遊具ができるのか完成まで子ども達には内緒にしている園もあります。内緒にしている場合は、子ども達とのちょっとした会話にも注意が必要となります。何も話せないのは心苦しいですが（笑）。

問題がなければ、子ども達の質問に答えています。遊具の完成が待てない子どもに、余った板切れを使って簡易的なすべり台をつくってあげたらとても喜んでくれました。

また現場は子ども達が普通に生活している場でもあるので、お昼寝のある園では、その時間帯になるべく大きな音を出す作業をしないように配慮しています。

園のみんなから大きな「ありがとう」

新潟県新潟市にある栄光幼稚園での話ですが、工事が終わり園に遊具の引き渡しをする時に園からサプライズがありました。子ども達全員が整列したかと思うと、スタッフ全員に対して感謝状の授与式を行ってくれたんです。

園のみなさんからの「ありがとう」という気持ちと笑顔がうれしくて、こういう時に仕事のやりがいを感じますね。

これからもアネビーの遊具で遊び、学び、たくさんの思い出をつくってくれたらと思います。

Our Priority

Making safe equipment that promotes development is our goal. We ensure that the equipment is the safe size, and confirm that there are no parts that may cause injury. After work that generates metal chips, we use magnets to remove them.

Construction and installation can create hazards for children, so we pay the utmost attention to tool and site management and safety.

Manufacturing and Children

Teachers' explanations to children about the construction differ from school to school. Some schools share the excitement by showing the designs to the children and explain the equipment. Some keep it secret until construction is complete. When they do, we need to be careful in their conversations with children. It is sometimes difficult not to let the cat out of the bag.

Children ask us many questions. We answer as best we can without spoiling the surprise. Once we made a temporary slide with the left-over materials for a child who was very sad at not being able to use the slide during construction. The child was so happy.

Children take naps every day at the schools, so we do our best work quietly during naptime.

Appreciation from Children

When we finished construction at Eiko Kindergarten in Niigata, we were surprised when all the children lined up and gave us thank-you notes.

That was a great surprise for us. We felt so happy about their appreciation and enjoyed seeing their smiles. These are the moments that make us know that our work is important.

The children who play on our equipment will learn and make lots of memories that will stay with them as they grow into their future.

一人ひとり違うデザインの感謝状／Thank-you notes

改装され立派になった「わんぱくとりで」の前で授与式／Opening the refurbished fortress (*Wanpaku Toride*)

【第3章】
園庭を組み立てる
[Chapter III]
Structuring the Playgarden

「園庭」を構成し、子ども達の育ちに有効な要素とはなんでしょう？
園庭は外にあり、天候や時間、また四季の移ろいなど同じ場所でも刻々と変化していきます。
だから子ども達は、その変化にも心ときめかせ、対応力を身につけ育っていくのです。
ここでは『園庭を組み立てる』をテーマに、さまざまな「やってみたい」を生み出す要素を
紹介します。

What elements structure the playgarden and promote the effective growth of individual children ?
Playgardens are outside and change moment to moment along with the weather, time, and season.
Children are excited about the changes, and these changes help them develop their ability to
adjust to the environment.
In this chapter, we introduce important elements of playgarden structure that motivate activity.

さまざまな「やってみたい」を生み出す要素
Elements that motivate activity

- ■ 築山
  Hill
- ■ じゃぶじゃぶ池（ガチャポンプ）
  Jabu Jabu Pond (Gacha Pump)
- ■ ビオトープ
  Biotope
- ■ 砂場 & だいもれ
  Sand Pool & Daimore
- ■ デッキ（こもれび、勾玉など）
  Deck (Sunshine, Small Jewel, etc.)
- ■ ツリーデッキ
  Tree Deck
- ■ ゆりかごスウィング
  Cradle Swing
- ■ 空中ケーブル
  Aerial Cable
- ■ トランポリン
  Trampoline
- ■ ゴーカートコース
  Go-kart Course
- ■ 石垣・忍者小屋
  Stone Wall & Ninja Hut
- ■ 植栽 パーゴラ
  Planting & Pergola
- ■ 植栽計画
  Planting Plan
- ■ スカイシェード
  SKY Shades
- ■ ランダムフェンス
  Random Fence
- ■ 小さな小屋とみちくさデッキ
  Small Hut & Michikusa Deck
- ■ 水遊び小屋
  Water Play Cottage
- ■ 高床式どろだんご小屋
  Raised-Floor-Style Hut for Mud Ball Making
- ■ ネットの海
  The Net Sea
- ■ 夢のかけ橋
  Bridge of Dreams

■築山／Hill

からだ全体を使った「のぼる」、「おりる」は、体力とバランス感覚を向上させる基本的な要素です。

Going up and down requires the entire body, and this movement improves physical fitness and sense of balance.

芝の築山、土の築山、空を眺める場所 ─── 坂戸富士見幼稚園／埼玉県坂戸市
Lawn Hill & Soil Hill – The place to see the sky –Sakado Fujimi Kindergarten/ Sakado City, Saitama Prefecture

サクラの木の下に広がる芝と土の築山を駆け回り、デッキでくつろぐ。また砂場で泥だんごを作り、遊具を果敢に登り降りする。この遊び場のおかげで、最近ではマラソン大会であごを上げる子が少なくなったと、子ども達の成長に大きな変化を先生方も実感しているそうです。
Children run on the lawn and soil hills under cherry trees and rest on the deck. They rush to the sand pool to make mud balls, and climb on the playgarden equipment. Thanks to this playgarden, the children's stamina has increased. Teachers have noticed significant changes like this in the children's growth.

芝の築山は、みんなで寝っ転がって空を眺める場所。デッキではお弁当も食べる／The lawn hill is where the children lie down to look at the sky. Children enjoy eating lunch on the deck.

次々と楽しみが見つけられる場所 ─── 冨士見保育園／東京都立川市
The place where children find one fun thing to do after another – Fujimi Nursery School/ Tachikawa City, Tokyo

「砂遊び」と「水遊び」の要素をバランスよくもっている築山は、その他にもバランス感覚が試されたり、かがむ姿勢を覚えたり、お片づけを身につけたりと遊びの要素が盛りだくさんの場所です。
The hill has well-balanced elements of both sand and water play. It also helps children to develop their sense of balance, and learn bending postures and how to clean up. It has a wide variety of the elements of play.

上から見ると、この築山だけでも十分回遊して遊べることがわかる／Looking down the hill, you can see many chances for children to play.

小さな冒険心を満たす ─── 光明第一・光明第三保育園／東京都八王子市
Satisfying children's spirit of adventure –Koumyou Daiichi&Daisan Nursery School/ Hachioji City, Tokyo

どちらの築山にも小さい子達がいつもいっぱい集まってきます。第一保育園にはシーサーが子ども達の冒険心を待ち構えています。また第三保育園は半分が野草で覆われていて土と草花の両方を楽しむことができます。
Children enjoy playing around both hills. At Daiichi Nursery School, a Shisa (Okinawan lion) statue awaits the adventurous children. Half of the land at Daisan Nursery School is covered with wild plants, and the other half is soil. Children can enjoy both soil and flowers.

第三保育園／Daisan Nursery School　　　第一保育園／Daiichi Nursery School

【第3章】園庭を組み立てる

心ゆくまで泥んこになる — ぽらりすこども園／群馬県前橋市
Children always enjoy playing in mud – Porarisu Preschool/ Maebashi City, Gunma Prefecture

上から水を流したら子ども達に大人気の「どろんこスライダー」に大変身。てっぺんには上から潜れる縦トンネルがあり、中腹にあいた横トンネルと合流することができる不思議な築山です。
Pouring water from the top, it becomes a "mud slide." A vertical tunnel starts from the top, and merges with a horizontal tunnel in the middle. The children enjoy this hill very much.

築山のてっぺんにあるもぐら穴。下から見たら何でできているかわかるかな？／ A mole burrow on the top of the hill. This is the inside of the mole burrow seen from the bottom. Can you tell what the material is?

挑戦への初めのステップ — 昭和女子大学附属 昭和こども園／東京都世田谷区
The first step to new challenges – Showa Women's University Showa Kodomoen/ Setagaya-ku, Tokyo

「空飛ぶ船（ツリーデッキ）」の前に「くじらとう」と名付けられた土と芝の築山。そこはまるで森の中。自然の中で遊ばせたいと植えられたたくさんの植栽が、日々、子ども達と一緒に育ってきています。
A lawn and soil hills named *Kujirato* (whale tower) are placed in front of the Flying Ship (tree deck). It looks like a forest. A wide variety of trees and plants that provide a natural environment grow daily along with the children.

築山から続く遊具へ、子ども達の挑戦はとどまることなく続く／ Children move from the hill to the play equipment searching for something new.

「築山」基本設計　Basic Design of the Hill

築山は山砂で仕上げた「土」の築山。また、こも芝や雑草、人工芝で仕上げた「芝」の築山。そして自然木を組み合わせたり、石や岩を景観の中に取り入れたり、バリエーションは尽きません。園の気候条件などにも合わせることが可能です。表面をカバーしない「土」の築山は、土台部分を赤土などの安定した土質のもので整形・填圧し、表土には山砂を中心とした遊びやすい砂を、遊びの目的や地域に合わせて選んでいます。

There are two hills, one is made of soil and sand, and the other is covered with natural and artificial lawn, and wild plants. We can combine these with different natural elements such as trees, rocks, and stones. It is also possible to adjust to the weather of the region. The soil hill's base is formed with stable and firm soil such as red clay covered by mountain sand, material that is easy to play with. We choose different materials in accordance with the purpose of play and regional conditions.

円乗寺保育園／Enjoji Nursery School

福井佼成幼稚園／Fukui Kosei Kindergarten

■じゃぶじゃぶ池（ガチャポンプ）
/Jabu Jabu Pond (Gacha Pump)

思い切り水と戯れる楽しさは、子ども達の特権。水や木や土に直接ふれることで、豊かな創造力と感性を養います。

Children love playing with water. Coming into direct contact with water, trees, and soil cultivates imagination and sensitivity.

水と土が融合する園庭――― 渋川あゆみ保育園／滋賀県草津市
A playgarden integrating water and soil – Shibukawa Ayumi Nursery School/ Kusatsu City, Shiga Prefecture

ヨーロッパの石畳を連想させるじゃぶじゃぶ池と水流れ。築山での土遊びと水遊びを組み合わせて、単純な泥だんごづくりから、水を使った地形を変化させる遊びへと遊びの質が変化していきます。
Jabu Jabu Pond and the flow of water remind us of European stone pavement. Combining activities using water and soil at the hills, children shift from making mud balls, which is simple, to forming mini-mountains and rivers, which is more complicated.

左／じゃぶじゃぶ池。右／手押しのガチャポンプは小さい子にも大人気。井戸水や雨水を貯めておけば災害時のトイレや洗濯にも使うことができる／ (Left) Jabu Jabu Pond (Right) The hand-operated Gacha Pump is very popular with small children too. Stored rain and well water is convenient for clothes washing and use for restrooms during disaster.

水流れ／ Water Flow

棚田のような竜の池――― 幼保連携型認定こども園 円福幼稚園／長野県長野市
Dragon Pond looks like a terraced rice-field –
Certified Center for Early Childhood Education, Enpuku Kindergarten/ Nagano City, Nagano Prefecture

冬期湛水不耕起栽培農法の田んぼビオトープを通して関わってきた自然を、もっと身近に感じられ、水遊びができる場所にしたいという思いからできあがったじゃぶじゃぶ池です。
Enpuku Kindergarten has created a biotope in the rice field by filling it with water during winter to attract life. The kindergarten wanted to utilize this natural environment to create a place in which children could play with water. Jabu Jabu Pond was made with their wish as a guide.

左／生きもの達がいっぱいの田んぼビオトープ。右／モザイクタイルで描かれた民話「竜の子太郎」をはじめ、園長先生自ら遊び場に物語を創り出している／ (Left) Biotope and the rice fields teeming with a variety of life. (Right) Children are surrounded by the story, Taro the Dragon Boy, including a scene of the story described with mosaic tiles.

築山から始まった水遊び――― 小立野善隣館こども園／石川県金沢市
Water activities starting from the hill – Kodatsuno Zenrinkan Kodomoen/ Kanazawa City, Ishikawa Prefecture

子どもは水も土もすごく好き。子どもだけではなく、先生方が泥んこ遊びをさせたいと思わせる環境をつくりたいという想いから、築山の隣に池と砂場を併設した水遊び場ができました。
Children love to play with water and soil. Teachers also wanted to create an environment in which children could play with mud. They realized their dream by creating a spot to play that features a pond and sand pool next to a hill.

池の周りは大きな石で囲まれ迫力満点／ The pond is surrounded by large stones. Children enjoy the thrill and play enthusiastically.

【第3章】園庭を組み立てる

水湧き出す「さくらじま」 ───円乗寺保育園／鹿児島県姶良郡湧水町
Gushing Water from the top of Mt. Sakurajima–Enjoji Nursery School/ Yusui-cho, Aira-gun, Kagoshima Prefecture

鹿児島という土地柄、身近な桜島と錦江湾のイメージを取り入れた「さくらじま」。山のてっぺんや丸太から湧き出す水は子ども達に大人気です。

The school made a miniature Mt. Sakurajima and Kinko Bay. The water gushing from the top of the mountain and between logs is very popular with children.

子ども達見守る200年の歴史 ───嵯峨幼稚園／京都府京都市
200 years of history watching over the children–Saga Kindergarten/ Kyoto City, Kyoto Prefecture

樹齢推定200年以上の大きなアラカシを囲んだじゃぶじゃぶ池。中央にはお地蔵さんが見守っており、「じぞう池」として親しまれています。

Jabu Jabu Pond was built around a large quercus glauca tree believed to be more than 200 years old. A guardian deity of children (jizo) sits in the middle. Therefore, it is also fondly called Jizo Pond.

旧園舎で使われていた鬼瓦と瓦を活用した水流れはまるで龍の背中／The water flows into a pond made of ridge-end and regular tiles used at the former kindergarten building. It looks like a dragon's back.

「じゃぶじゃぶ池」基本設計   Basic Design of Jabu Jabu Pond

ガチャポンプを併設したタイプから、砂場や築山を組み合わせて泥んこ遊びを楽しめるものまで、さまざまな自然遊びを体験することができます。

Jabu Jabu Pond has wide variations. It can be combined with a Gacha Pump or a sand pool and hills to give the children the opportunity to play with mud. All types provide the children with chances to experience a wide range of activities in nature.

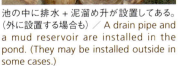

池の中に排水＋泥溜め升が設置してある。（外に設置する場合も）／A drain pipe and a mud reservoir are installed in the pond. (They may be installed outside in some cases.)

■ビオトープ / Biotope

生きものを観察し、愛でる気持ちが育ちます。
心休まる自然とのふれあいも、子どもの情緒を豊かにします。

A biotope helps develop the children's ability to observe as they learn to love nature and the life that lives in it. Being surrounded by nature helps children to develop emotionally.

蛍が飛び交うビオトープ —— 帝塚山学院幼稚園／大阪府大阪市
A biotope where fireflies live – Tezukayama Gakuin Kindergarten/ Osaka City, Osaka Prefecture

21世紀を生きる子ども達に大切な資質は「豊かな感性」であるとの想いから、自然がその力を育んでくれるようにと、自然池を再現しました。するとさまざまな植物が美しく光る蛍の育成に適する状態までになりました。大阪市内で蛍が見られる稀有な場所は、園長先生の維持管理の賜物です。
Having strong sensibilities is an important quality for children living in the 21st century to develop. This kindergarten built a natural-looking pond with trees and plants. Now a wide variety of plants nurture beautiful fireflies. Supported by the principal's loving care, this kindergarten has become one of the rare spots in Osaka City where fireflies can be seen.

水源は水道水だがポンプアップ方式を採用し、ランニングコストにも考慮した／ Reducing costs utilizing the pump system for tap water.

身近な水辺は癒しと学びの場 —— 関西国際学園／兵庫県神戸市
Water play area where children relax and learn – Kansai International Academy Kindergarten/ Kobe City, Hyogo Prefecture

デッキが備えられている癒しのエリアにビオトープは設置されています。じゃかご（金属メッシュかご）に自然石を詰めたフェンスは爬虫類や昆虫の住処となるのと同時に景観を整えます。
A biotope is located in a relaxing area equipped with a deck. A metal mesh basket filled with stones serves as a home for reptiles and insects.

使われている自然石は地元六甲山で採取されたもの／ The stones in the basket were gathered at nearby Mt. Rokko.

自然池と同じつくりをしているため、天候や生物の状況により、自然の変化と同じような現象が起こる／ Because the pond has the same structure as a natural pond, the weather and life influence it.

かっぱが見守るお池 —— 大森みのり幼稚園／東京都大田区
A pond watched over by a Kappa (legendary water animal) – Omori Minori Kindergarten/ Ota-ku, Tokyo

春夏秋冬、池の周りの植物がちょっとずつ変化していくのも楽しみのひとつです。
Small changes in the plants around the pond each season are also exciting.

|「ビオトープ」基本設計　　Basic Design of Biotope

基本的には雨水を利用して、12〜13cmの浅い水辺となります。小さなスペースでも設置でき、たくさんの植物を植えたり、魚や虫を観察することもできます。

The biotope is a shallow type 12 to 13 cm high utilizing rain water. This can be installed in a narrow space. Many plants can be planted, and fish and insects can be observed.

【第3章】園庭を組み立てる

■ 砂場 & だいもれ / Sand Pool & Daimore

「幼児期の遊び体験」を思う存分に。
創造力と共同作業が生まれて、子どもがどんどん育つ場所です。

Providing chances to experience important activities during childhood.
The sand pool and Daimore develop children's imagination and promote cooperative activities that contribute to their healthy growth.

自然に溶け込む棚田砂場 — 鶯谷さくら幼稚園／東京都渋谷区
Terraced sand pools blending with nature – Uguisudani Sakura Kindergarten/ Shibuya-ku, Tokyo

棚田のような砂場には、それぞれの子どもが自分のやりたいことを夢中になってやっています。時には同じ囲いの中で友達と、また囲いを越えての共同作業になったりと無限の世界が築かれています。
Terraced sand pools attract the children and encourage them to explore. Sometimes they play together in the same sand pool, or play among the different pools.

選べる砂で、遊びも広がる — 光明第一保育園／東京都八王子市
Choose different sand for different activities – Koumyou Daiichi Nursery School/ Hachioji City, Tokyo

みんなで協力しながらガチャポンプで水を引き込めば、泥んこ砂場のできあがり。この砂場は粘土性の高い山砂とさらさらの川砂の2つに仕切られていて子どもがやりたいと思う遊びを選ぶことができます。
Making water flow with the Gacha Pump, children can create a muddy sand pool. This sand pool is separated into two areas: one is mountain sand, which is more clayish, and the other is drier river sand. Children can choose sand according to the activity.

山砂×川砂×ガチャポンプの遊び —
調布多摩川幼稚園／東京都調布市
Mountain sand×River sand×Gacha Pump –
Chofu Tamagawa Kindergarten/ Chofu City, Tokyo

「もっともっと、遊び込める場所にしたい」と子ども達が夢中になる「自然遊び」に注目。ガチャポンプがつくり出す水流れと特徴の違う2種類の大きな砂山で子ども達はいろんな遊びを開発中です。
This kindergarten focused on activities in nature to create a playgarden that increases the children's enthusiasm. Children engage in a wide variety of activities with water from the Gacha Pump around two different types of large sand mountains.

お片づけしたくなる砂場 —
東京幼稚園／東京都大田区
A sand pool that teaches the joy of cleaning up –
Tokyo Kindergarten/ Ota-ku, Tokyo

隣家への砂塵の飛び散りなどを考慮して、ランダムフェンスを併設した砂場。遊び道具を楽しく収納でき、自信作の「泥だんご」の展示場所もあって、子ども達の人気の場所です。
The sand pool at this kindergarten has a fence made of randomly cut wooden boards to prevent the scattering of sand to neighboring houses. The area has a storage shed for tools, and shelves for mud balls that the children make. Children have fun cleaning up the tools.

■デッキ（こもれび、勾玉など）／Deck (Sunshine, Small Jewel, etc.)

デッキは小さい子ども達の遊び場であり、大きい子ども達のコミュニケーションと安らぎの場です。

The decks provide smaller children with a safe space to play, and older children with a place to relax and interact.

にぎやかな声が響くピアノデッキ ——— 松崎幼稚園／山口県防府市
A piano-shaped deck filled with the lively voices of children – Matsuzaki Kindergarten/ Hofu City, Yamaguchi Prefecture

上から見るとまるでグランドピアノのような形をしたデッキは、シンボルツリーと一体化した憩いの場。ドリームログをゆったりと楽しむことができ、きちんと収納できるスペースをデッキの奥につくり、お片づけも身につけられます。

Looking from above, this deck is in the shape of a grand piano. It provides children with a place of recreation and relaxation unified with the tree that symbolizes the kindergarten. They can relax and enjoy playing with the Dream Log. At the far end of the deck, a storage shed is placed so that children can naturally learn how to clean up tools.

グッドデザイン賞を受賞した講堂にある「ジャングルツリー」という名の挑戦する遊具もリノベーションされた／ A piece of play equipment named the Jungle Tree, which received the Good Design Award, is renovated at the main hall.

水遊びと融合した裸足の楽園 ——— 畦刈保育園／長崎県長崎市
A paradise where children can play with water in their bare feet – Azekari Nursery School/ Nagasaki City, Nagasaki Prefecture

広いデッキにはいつでも小さい子ども達の笑顔や歓声であふれています。また子ども達が集まる噴水からデッキに沿ってできた水流れは、じゃぶじゃぶ池へと続き楽しみは広がります。

The wide deck is always filled with the bright smiles and cheerful voices of small children. The water flows along the deck from the fountain where children gather, and it continues toward the Jabu Jabu Pond to create an exciting play environment.

夏はシェードを取り付けてプールのスペースに。ひと休みのベンチも／ Placing shade over the deck in summer provides a comfortable space in which the children can enjoy playing with water. Children can also take a rest on the bench.

「デッキ」基本設計　Basic Design of Deck

デッキは小さい子ども達が外の世界を感じながら安心して遊べるスペースとして、また大きい子ども達にとっては遊びの合間のひと休みや、お弁当を広げて友達との経験を共有する場としても重要なスペースとなります。シェードやフジ棚のパーゴラ、園のシンボルツリーの日陰を上手に利用して夏も快適な場所にすることができます。

The deck is an important space that allows small children to feel the outdoors and play safely in it. It is also important for older children to have a place to rest between activities and to enjoy eating lunch with their friends. Utilizing shade, a pergola with wisteria, and a symbol tree, we can create a comfortable summer space for children.

■ツリーデッキ／Tree Deck

園のシンボルツリーを遊び場に。
子ども達の成長を見守る自然と調和した遊具です。

Using a tree to create a place for children to play.
Great play equipment in harmony with nature watches the children grow.

愛されるツリーデッキ — 認定こども園 あゆのさと／静岡県伊豆市
A tree deck that the children love – Certified Center for Early Childhood Education, Ayunosato/ Izu City, Shizuoka Prefecture

大きな2本のケヤキを中心にしたツリーデッキを熱望された園長先生。ひとつは大きなすべり台、もうひとつは空中回廊をもつツリーデッキ。さらに二塔を結び、砂場も加えて多彩な遊び場になりました。

The principal's dream was to build a tree deck around two large zelkova trees growing at the school. One became a large slide, and the other became a deck with an air corridor. Connecting two pieces of play equipment created a spot for a wide range of activities.

木登り、虫取り、滑り降りなどいろんな挑戦が待っている／ Lots of challenges such as climbing the trees, catching bugs, and sliding down await the children.

空中に飛び出す爽快感
清水保育園／宮崎県西都市
The feeling of joy that comes with jumping into the air –
Kiyomizu Nursery School/ Saito City, Miyazaki Prefecture

船首から子ども達が次々とジャンプ。立ったまま飛び降りるのが怖くて、座った体勢から降りる子もいますが、空中へ飛び出す爽快感を知った子は何回も挑戦しています。

One after another the children jump from a bow. Some children are afraid of jumping from a standing position; but, once they experience the joy of jumping into the air, they try over and over again.

上のデッキまで行くと今まで体験したことのない遠くの景色まで見渡すことができる／ From the upper deck, they can see far-away scenery that they have not yet experienced.

つくりたかったのは自然の遊び場
押原こども園／山梨県中巨摩郡昭和町
Wanting to build a playgarden surrounded by nature –
Oshihara Kodomoen/ Showa-cho, Nakakoma-gun, Yamanashi Prefecture

20数年前、木々を植え、石を置いた「自然の遊び場」は危険だとの声により一時断念しましたが、大きく育った木々と一体化したツリーデッキをつくることで、石庭の趣をもつ園庭となりました。

More than 20 years ago, the plan to make a playgarden surrounded by nature by planting trees and placing stones was once given up due to some voices that it might be dangerous for the children. But now, the tree deck unified with the grown trees and created a stone garden-like playgarden.

木々の間に張られたロープを伝って、縦横無尽に遊びが回遊していく／ Moving hand over hand along a rope placed between trees, children move freely around the playgarden.

そこは小さな子ども達の森 — 昭和女子大学附属 昭和こども園／東京都世田谷区
A forest filled with small children –
Showa Women's University Showa Kodomoen/ Setagaya-ku, Tokyo

大きな窓ガラスから光が差し込み、都心にありながら自然豊かな新園舎。そこから園庭を見るとたくさんの木々に囲まれた「空飛ぶ船」「くじらとう」と名付けられたツリーデッキと築山、そして子ども達の姿が、まるで大きな絵画のごとく鮮やかに浮かび上がります。そんな森の中の秘密基地に子ども達は毎日、夢中です。

Although located in the middle of Tokyo, this school is filled with sunlight coming through large windows, and it is surrounded by a wealth of nature. Looking at the playgarden from inside the school, we can see a flying ship surrounded by trees, a tree deck named *Kujirato* (whale tower), hills, and children as if it were a lively scene from a large painting. The children enjoy this secret base created in the forest.

「ツリーデッキ」基本設計　Basic Design of Tree Deck

園庭を有効活用するためにも、園で大切に育んできたシンボルツリーを避けてしまうのではなく、より子ども達に愛される存在として遊具と一体化するのがツリーデッキです。自然木に近い白木でつくれば森で遊ぶような遊具となり、HAGSの素材と融合させれば今までにない新しいシンボルへと変化します。

To utilize the playgarden effectively, a tree deck can be built around a symbol tree. The deck incorporates the tree and becomes a favorite place to play. If the deck is built with plain wood, children can feel as if they were playing in a forest. If the deck is built with HAGS materials, the deck becomes a new symbol of the school.

■ゆりかごスウィング／Cradle Swing

「揺れる」感覚は、バランス感覚とリズム感を育てます。

Swinging is a great way for children to develop their sense of balance and rhythm.

コンパクトで限られたスペースにも設置可能な「ゆりかごスウィング」。遊びはじめの子ども達には大人が優しく揺らすことで、安心して楽しむことができます。また複数の子ども達が乗る人と漕ぐ人を順番にするなど、自主的に自分たちのルールを作っていくコミュニケーションの場にもなります。

The Cradle Swing can be installed in a compact space. Adults can help children who have just started playing with the equipment. Children also have the chance to interact and make their own rules, rules such as who rides first and who pushes the swing.

【第3章】園庭を組み立てる

太陽第一幼稚園／神奈川県川崎市
Taiyo Daiichi Kindergarten/
Kawasaki City, Kanagawa Prefecture

立正佼成会附属 佼成育子園／東京都杉並区
Rissho Koseikai Kosei Ikujien/
Suginami-ku, Tokyo

大森みのり幼稚園／東京都大田区
Omori Minori Kindergarten/
Ota-ku, Tokyo

松本幼稚園／東京都江戸川区
Matsumoto Kidergarten/
Edogawa-ku, Tokyo

認定こども園 福井佼成幼稚園／福井県福井市
Certified Center for Early Childhood Education,
Fukui Kosei Kindergarten/ Fukui City, Fukui Prefecture

■空中ケーブル / Aerial Cable

空中へ飛び出していく子ども達の顔は、
みんな誇らしげです。

When children jump into the air, they look very proud.

高い場所から自分で飛び出して、低い場所へと一気に滑り降りてくる空中ケーブルは、子ども達にとって他のどんな遊具よりも大きな勇気が必要となります。さらに持続的な握力・腹筋力・背筋力など挑戦する自分の力を見極め、これまでより高い経験値を目指す遊びとして位置づけられます。最後まで掴まっていられるか、上手に着地できるか、これまでの遊びの成果を総動員して挑戦するご褒美でもあります。そして滑走時の爽快感と、着地した時の達成感は子ども達の大きな喜びとなるでしょう。

Of all the playgarden equipment, this aerial cable helps the children develop the courage to jump. It also helps children develop the strength in their hands, abdomen, and back to achieve ability that surpasses their earlier development. Their reward is the ability to enjoy to the fullest the strength and ability they have developed through activities on the playgarden. They are both excited and anxious about holding onto the cable until the end, and whether they will be able to jump and land. After they complete the activity, their sense of fulfilment and strength give them great pleasure.

小立野善隣館こども園／石川県金沢市
Kodatsuno Zenrinkan Kodomoen/ Kanazawa City, Ishikara Prefecture

この空中ケーブルは3つの塔を制覇したものだけが挑戦できる特権。最初のチャレンジでは、怖くてためらってしまう子もいます。でも1回でも空中へ飛び出して行った子は、この空中ケーブルの虜になります。何度でも何度でも挑戦している姿は、みんな本当に楽しそうで実に誇らしげです。そして次の勇者のためにシートを手渡しに行くのも、みんなで決めた大切なルールです。

This aerial cable awaits those who have scaled the three towers. On their first attempt, some children are reluctant to jump. However, the children who jump on their first try become thoroughly fascinated by the activity. The children who jump many times look very pleased and proud. The children also made the rule to hand over the seat to the next child in line.

大森みのり幼稚園／東京都大田区
Omori Minori Kindergarten/ Ota-ku, Tokyo

東京の住宅街の中とは思えないほど、植栽が豊かに茂り、色とりどりの花やさまざまな実がなる「ふたつ山」。その中でも一番、野性味あふれる遊具がこの空中ケーブルです。この場所には年長さんだけではなく、2歳児も遊びに来ます。すると空中ケーブルに挑戦しようとする子ども達が続出。まだ掴まる力と自分の体を加速する中で保持する力が不十分でも、大人の補佐で悠々と遊んでいます。

The Twin Peaks at this kindergarten are surrounded by a wealth of trees and filled with different colored flowers and fruit. The wildest equipment at Twin Peaks is this aerial cable. The aerial cable is not only popular among the older children, it's also popular with the 2 year olds. The children are eager to try jumping into the air with this cable. Younger children lack grip strength at accelerated speed, but they also enjoy this cable with help from the adults.

■ トランポリン／Trampoline

トランポリンでぴょんぴょん跳ねる感覚は思いのままに自分の体を動かし、リズム感が育つ基本となります。

Jumping on the trampoline helps children to develop the ability to move their bodies rhythmically.

平安保育園／香川県高松市

Heian Nursery School/
Takamatsu City, Kagawa Prefecture

HAGSの遊具の上部に組み込むことで、上まで登ることができたご褒美として楽しいトランポリンを体験できます。
Assembled with the upper part of the HAGS play equipment, children can experience a fun trampoline as a reward for climbing to the top.

ハイジアパーク南陽／山形県南陽市

Hygeia Park Nanyo/
Nanyo City, Yamagata Prefecture

立正佼成会附属 佼成育子園／東京都杉並区

Rissho Koseikai Kosei Ikujien/
Suginami-ku, Tokyo

地面や床に近いため、小さい子でも遊ぶことができ、踏むと沈む感覚や、ふわふわ揺れる感覚を経験することができます。屋内、屋外問わず、対応できます。
The trampoline at this school is low to the ground, which allows small children to enjoy sinking into it and swinging on it. It can be used both indoors and out.

アネビートリムパークお台場／東京都江東区

Aneby Trimpark Odaiba/ Koto-ku, Tokyo

独立型のトランポリンで屋内での使用になります。大きく跳んでも囲いがあるため安全です。また人数も規制できるため子ども達に順番を守ることや、他の子ども達の跳ぶ姿を見て学習する機会もあります。
It is an independent-type trampoline for indoor use. It is enclosed for safety. The number of children that can use it at one time is limited, and this helps them learn how to wait their turn as they see how to jump by watching others.

|「トランポリン」基本設計　Basic Design of Trampoline

トランポリンは手軽な有酸素運動です。最初は小さなジャンプでも、ただ歩くだけでも構いません。気が向いた時に遊んでいると、やがて上手に跳べる様になります。楽しみながら体幹を鍛え、美しい姿勢とリズミカルな身のこなしを身につけましょう。生後12ヶ月くらいでも上を歩きます。18ヶ月ごろからは、ジャンプして遊ぶことができます。HAGSの遊具に組み込むタイプ、地面に設置するタイプ、室内用としての独立型のタイプがあります。

The trampoline is very useful for aerobic exercise. First, children can start by walking or low jumping. As they play at their own pace, they develop the ability to jump higher over time. Children can strengthen their trunks, develop proper posture and rhythmical movement while they play. Children can walk on it at about 12 months and jump on it at about 18 months. The trampoline can be combined with other HAGS equipment for outside use, and the independent-type can be used inside.

■ゴーカートコース／Go-kart Course

乗り物に乗る楽しさだけではない、子どもの心の成長も育みます。

Go-karts are not just fun, they also promote emotional growth.

足を使って乗り物を前に進める、さらにペダルを漕ぐという動きは、足をしっかりと踏み込むことを繰り返さないとできない初めての子どもにとってはとても難しい動きです。つまり自分と乗り物を支えて押し出す力と、その動作を継続できる筋力、そして全身のバランス感覚などたくさんの身体能力が必要となります。また乗り物を安全に楽しむには遊ぶための環境を整えることも重要です。「一方向で走る」など遊びながらルールを守る大切さを学ぶことで社会性を身につけたり、レースを開催して仲間との協調性を育てていきます。

Pushing or pedaling to make the go-kart move is a challenge for small children that requires repeated practice. They also develop physical abilities. For example, they develop the strength to push the karts, the stamina to maintain movement, and a sense of balance. Providing a safe place in which the children can develop these abilities requires that adults create the appropriate environment. Kart races help children learn the importance of following rules and cooperating with others.

大森みのり幼稚園／東京都大田区
Omori Minori Kindergarten/ Ota-ku, Tokyo

園庭のひとつ「ふたつ山」にあるゴーカートコースは木々の間を抜け、起伏のある道を走る、まるで自然の山をサイクリングするような爽快さが自慢のコースです。まだ漕ぐことが覚束ない子ども達が「がたがた道」に果敢に挑戦する姿や、自然と始まる競争、逆にのんびりと走ることを楽しむ子もいて、コースはいつも盛況です。

The Go-kart Course at Twin Peaks runs through trees with rises and falls along the way. It is very invigorating, like cycling in the mountains. Some are still learning how to pedal. They try hard to go up the rises. Some start races with others, and some just enjoy riding in the kart. The Go-kart Course is always filled with children.

アネビートリムパークお台場／東京都江東区
Aneby Trimpark Odaiba/ Koto-ku, Tokyo

ゴーカートコースには、ペダルを漕いで、ハンドルを操作し、ブレーキで止まり、ルールを守って乗るという、子ども達が「身体感覚を養うこと」と「感情をコントロールすること」を同時に育てていくための要素がたくさんつまっています。またライセンスカードなどを作って「できたこと」を明確にし、子ども達の意欲と達成感を高めることができます。

The Go-kart Course has many elements that help children to develop their physical abilities. These include the movement of pedaling, steering, and breaking. In addition to developing physical abilities, they also learn how to control their emotions and follow rules. Children who complete the course receive a license, which recognizes their achievement, increases their sense of accomplishment, and motivates them to accept greater challenges.

■石垣・忍者小屋／Stone Wall & Ninja Hut

難しければ難しいほど達成感は格別です。

The more challenging it is, the more fulfilling it feels.

子ども達の「挑戦したい」という意欲を最大限に引き出す石垣と忍者小屋。ここは自分の力だけが頼りになります。まずどこに手をかけて登り始めるかを考えたら、最初に両手で自分を引き上げ、次には裸足で踏み心地を確認しながら踏ん張って自分自身を押し上げていく、その工程を繰り返します。この石垣と忍者小屋を攻略した子ども達は本物の忍者のよう。「達成感」を心と体に蓄えてたくましくなっていきます。

The stone wall and Ninja Hut help maximize the children's motivation to try. They rely on their own abilities and need to think about where to put their hands to start climbing. They need to push themselves up with both hands, and place their bare feet to push up farther. Climbing up the stone wall and reaching the Ninja Hut makes the children mentally and physically stronger and gives them a sense of fulfillment.

認定こども園 福井佼成幼稚園／福井県福井市

Certified Center for Early Childhood Education, Fukui Kosei Kindergarten/ Fukui City, Fukui Prefecture

隠れ里のような佇まいの「にんじゃのさと」。石垣を登って辿り着く忍者屋敷にも、まだまだ挑戦の仕掛けがたくさんあります。子ども達は自分の手と足を思う存分駆使して2階へ。そして2階からは安定しないロープを伝って降りてきます。見晴らしのいい小屋からはハギのトンネルが美しいすべり台を楽しんで、また新しい遊びへと走っていきます。

Ninja no Sato (Ninja Village) has hiding places for the little Ninjas. Reached by climbing a stone wall, the Ninja Hut offers many activities for the children. Children use their hands and feet to climb to the second level. From the upper level, they descend using a rope. From the hut, which offers a nice view, the children enjoy a slide with a beautiful bush clover tunnel that brings them to the first level and onto the next activity.

勇者は満面の笑顔を見せてくれた／Adventurous child with a big smile

大森みのり幼稚園／東京都大田区

Omori Minori Kindergarten/ Ota-ku, Tokyo

子ども達の目の前にそびえ立つ「忍者山」とそのてっぺんにある「忍者小屋」。見上げる石垣に子ども達が怯むかと思えば、次から次へと足を掛けて我先にとてっぺんへ。そして誇らしげな顔で小屋の中を走り回っています。帰りは気分爽快なすべり台。もう終わりかなと思いきや、また石垣に足を掛けて子ども達の挑戦は続きます。

Ninja Mountain rises high before the children and Ninja Hut sits at the top. Children are eager to climb the stone wall and rush to the top. They run around in the hut triumphantly. They ride the thrilling slide down, and clamber up the stone wall again and again.

鳴子を打つのは勝者の証／The clapper signals the winner.

【第3章】園庭を組み立てる

■ 植栽 パーゴラ / Planting & Pergola

子ども達の豊かな心を育む「自然」。
四季を知り、実りを祝う心が育まれます。
木と暮らすことは「生きる」基本を学ぶことです。

Children grow through contact with nature.
They feel the changes that come with the passing of seasons and come to enjoy the harvest. Living with trees and nature teaches them the basic principles of life.

フジの木を見渡す遊び場 ―― 浦和みずほ幼稚園／埼玉県さいたま市
A playgarden wrapped around wisteria – Urawa Mizuho Kindergarten/ Saitama City, Saitama Prefecture

フジの木を活かした遊具では、遊びながら季節ごとに変化するフジの木とともに子ども達の成長もどんどん変化していきます。遊具のてっぺんには、辿りついた勇者だけが鳴らすことができる鐘があり、続々と鳴らす子が増えています。また途中までしか行けない子も自信をつけ、鉄棒や食事で頑張る姿を見せてくれるようになりました。

Children grow with the wisteria as they climb on the playgarden equipment. There is a bell at the top for children to ring. One after another, the children ring the bell. Even children who cannot reach the top gain confidence to try again and again. They are so motivated to try other things such as the bars, and the activity gives even the pickiest of eaters a hardy appetite.

自分たちだけの世界で安らぐ ―― 清泉インターナショナル学園／東京都世田谷区
Feeling comfortable with friends – Seisen International School/ Setagaya-ku, Tokyo

靴を脱いでデッキに上がるだけで、普段の生活とはちょっと違う空間が生まれます。そしてそこは女の子同士のお話をしたり、くつろぐことが安心してできる場所になります。自然の中だからこそ、会話も心も弾みます。

Taking off their shoes and resting on the deck, the children have a fun time in this wonderful space. The girls in particular love to relax and chat with their friends. They have lively conversations surrounded by nature.

こもれびの下で遊び、憩う ―― いじゅういんきた保育園／鹿児島県日置市
Play and relax in the sunshine that streams through the foliage – Ijuin-kita Nursery School/ Hioki City, Kagoshima Prefecture

砂場で遊ぶ子ども達は、自分の創作に没頭しているため、パーゴラによって強い日差しが緩和されるこの場所は、日射病の予防にもつながります。新しく設置されたガチャポンプでの水遊びや日陰でそよ風に吹かれる爽快さは、子ども達の心にゆとりを与えてくれるようです。

Children playing in the sand pool concentrate on what they are doing and do not think about the sun. The pergola covering the sand pool at this school helps cut the sun to protect the children. The gentle breeze and a newly installed Gacha Pump cool the children while they play in the shade.

五感で季節を感じる園庭 ——— かえで保育園／大阪府寝屋川市
A playgarden where children feel the seasons – Kaede Nursery School/ Neyagawa City, Osaka Prefecture

平らな園庭には遊びの変化が生まれなかったことから、斜面や水場を取り入れ、さらに自然の営みを五感で感じられる木々をたくさん植えました。その木々に咲く花や実りに子ども達は興味深々。香りがある花、色が変化する葉は遊びのアイテムとしても子ども達に喜ばれています。

The former playgarden was level, so the school decided to create slopes and water areas. The school also planted many trees so that the children could feel the seasonal changes.
Children are very interested in the flowers and fruit on the trees. Some flowers are fragrant, and some leaves change colors. These make good items for playtime activities.

「生きもの」の営みを知る ——— 昭和女子大学附属 昭和こども園／東京都世田谷区
Learning the cycle of life – Showa Women's University Showa Kodomoen/ Setagaya-ku, Tokyo

木を植える際、子ども達のための木陰だったり、木登りに挑戦したり、開花や実りの楽しさを感じられたりすることも大切です。さらにその場所にたくさんの木々が育つことで「緑の回廊」つまり新しく豊かな生態系が出現し、子ども達がそこでたくさんのことを学ぶことのできる場所になります。

This is an important element in planning for trees in a playgarden. Children can climb the trees, watch them come into blossom, and enjoy picking the fruit when it is ripe.
As trees grow, a new ecosystem develops. Green becomes part of the scenery, making it possible for the children to experience the preciousness of nature.

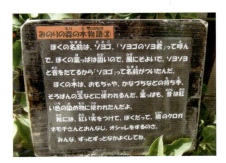

大きくなっても覚えていてね。

子どもの頃、覚えた木々や花々は楽しい思い出とともに、なかなか忘れられません。それは大人になってその子ども達にも受け継がれていく大切な「たからもの」。ぜひ子ども達に楽しく覚えてもらいましょう。

Good memories of trees and flowers.
The names of trees and flowers learned during childhood remain in our memory. These treasures will be passed down to the next generation too.

庭にあったクスノキをくりぬいて森の隠れ家ができた／ A camphor tree was hollowed out and made into a play space.

[第3章] 園庭を組み立てる

■植栽計画／Planting Plan

園庭を計画する上で、植栽計画はなくてはならないものです。3つのコンセプト『3本の木』計画を主とした、最適な植栽計画を紹介します。

A planting plan is essential for the design of a playgarden.
We introduce good planting plans based on the "Three Tree" concept.

『3本の木』計画

・1本は子どもたちのために
木を植えれば木陰が生まれ、夏の日差しから子どもたちを守ってくれます。
木登りしたり、ロープをかけてブランコしたり、ツリーデッキをつくったり、いろんな遊びの良き相棒となります。
花や食べられる実、きれいな紅葉、そして落葉。四季を通して様々な表情を見せる木々は、子ども達の五感を刺激し、感性を育みます。

・1本は鳥や虫たちのために
木を植えれば、土中の微生物から虫や鳥など、さまざまな生きものが集まってきます。
自然環境の破壊による生息場所が次第に失われる中、生きものの生息場所（ビオトープ）を創出して、
生物多様性を保全する取り組みは大事なテーマになります。また子ども達の身近な自然観察の場にもなります。

・1本は地域、地球のために
木々の緑は見る人の気持ちを豊かにしてくれます。近隣地域の方が心地よくなるように木々を植えましょう。
隣地境界沿いの木々は園庭内への視界を遮り、お互いのプライバシーを守る役割もあります。
地球の温暖化現象による気候変動の不安が高まる中、次世代を担う子ども達のため、地球の環境を守るため、木を植えましょう。

Three Tree Project

・One tree is for the children
Trees produce shade that protects children from the strong summer sunlight.
The trees are good playmates for children. They climb on them, enjoy swinging on ropes tied to them, and have fun at the tree deck.
The trees have beautiful flowers, bear delicious fruit, and show beautiful autumn leaves that change colors. These changes stimulate and develop the children's senses.

・One tree is for the birds and insects
Trees attract microorganisms in the ground, insects, birds, and many other forms of life.
Because habitats have been damaged by destruction of the natural environment, it is important to preserve biodiversity through the creation of biotopes. The biotopes also provide children with chances to observe nature.

・One tree is for the region and the earth
Trees calm and comfort us. Tree planting is a precious activity for the community too.
Trees become natural fences for the neighboring properties and protect privacy on both sides.
Climate change is causing concern, so let's plant trees to protect the global environment and the future for our children.

おすすめの植栽計画

植栽計画を考えるにあたって、おすすめの植栽計画を紹介します。
どんな木を植えたらいいか分からない、どんな植栽計画にすればいいのか分からない時などの参考にしてください。

Recommended Planting Plans

We show planting plans as a reference.
These plans show the kind of trees that are best for different locations and the best plans to make for them.

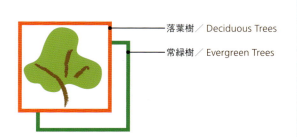
落葉樹／Deciduous Trees
常緑樹／Evergreen Trees

アイコンの説明／Icon Description

ドングリの木／Oak tree
きれいな花の木／Trees with Beautiful flowers
香（かおり）のよい木／Trees with Great Scent
きれいな紅葉の木／Trees with Beautiful Autumn Leaves
実のなる木（食べられる、鳥が来る）／Trees that Bear Fruits (Edible/ Eaten by Birds)
鳥や虫が集まる木／Trees where Birds and Insects Gather

雑木でつくる自然風の植栽計画
Natural plan with trees

かつて雑木林は子ども達の格好の遊び場でした。
そんな雑木林の雑木（ぞうき）を中心にした自然な植栽計画です。
Copses were once a magical place for children to play.
We introduce a planting plan using a copse as the main element.

●コナラ
花：4～5月 実：10～11月
クヌギと並び、雑木林の主要構成種で、ドングリの木。樹形は不整形で野趣に富んでおり、大きくなると重厚感を漂わせます。紅葉は黄色や赤色に変色し、派手さはないものの、趣があります。

Quercus Serrata
In bloom: April – May
Fruit: October – November
Quercus Serrata is one of the common choices for copse, and it produces acorns. The tree's shape is rather wild, and it creates an impressive atmosphere as it grows. The elegant leaves change to yellow and red in autumn.

●クヌギ
花：4～5月 実：10～11月
コナラと並び、雑木林の主要構成種で、ドングリの木。多くは単幹で、整った形の樹形です。甘い香りのする樹液にはカブトムシをはじめ、さまざまな夏の昆虫が集まります。

Sawtooth Oak
In bloom: April – May
Fruit: October – November
Sawtooth oak also produces acorns. The tree is mainly single-trunk and is balanced. The sap has a sweet scent that attracts beetles and other summer insects.

●エゴノキ
花：5月～6月 実：8～11月
クヌギ、コナラと同様、雑木林の構成種のひとつ。ベル型の花は下向きにつくので、子ども達の目線からも鑑賞できます。実は野鳥が好んで食べに来ます。

Japanese Snowbell
In bloom: May – June
Fruit: August – November
The Japanese snowbell's bell-shape flowers bloom downward, making them easy to see from the child's vantage point. Wild birds love the fruit.

●アカシデ
花：4～5月 実：8～10月
コナラ、クヌギ、エゴノキなどとともに雑木林の主要な構成種。葉や枝葉、姿形が細かく、明るく軽快な雑木林風を演出することができます。材はシイタケ栽培のホダ木、薪炭材として利用されます。

Carpinus Laxiflora
In bloom: April – May
Fruit: August – October
Carpinus Laxiflora is small, which makes it a great choice for a bright and light copse. The wood is used for firewood and as bed logs for mushroom cultivation.

●イヌシデ
花：4～5月
コナラ、クヌギ、エゴノキなどとともに雑木林の主要な構成種です。細く、すっきりと伸びた株立ちや、単幹物の寄植えが雑木の園庭に使われることが多い木。秋の黄葉が美しい。

Carpinus Tschonoskii
In bloom: April – May
Carpinus Tschonoskii's thin and slim form is popular and often used in group plantings of single-trunk trees.
The leaves changing to yellow in autumn are a beautiful sight.

第3章　園庭を組み立てる

シンボルツリーのある植栽計画
Planting Plan Featuring a Symbol Tree

狭い園庭でも大きなシンボルツリーが1本あるだけで、遊びが広がります。
ツリーデッキや木登り、ブランコ遊びなどに。
One symbol tree can expand the playgarden function in a small space.
The tree is used as a deck, for climbing, and for swings.

●クスノキ
花：5～6月 実：10～11月
巨樹の代表種。他の常緑樹に比べて葉色が明るく、全体の印象も爽やかで優美です。ムクドリやヒヨドリといった鳥も好んで果実を食べに来ます。
Camphor
In bloom: May – June
Fruit: October – November
Camphor is a common large tree. Compared with other evergreens, the leaves have a lighter color and the tree has a clean and elegant look. Starlings and bulbuls come to eat the fruit.

●ケヤキ
花：4～5月 実：10月
落葉広葉高木の中でも、高く幹回りも大きくなる雄大な木です。逆さホウキ状の樹形は独特で、冬季に一層目立ちます。新緑や黄葉も美しい木です。
Zelkova
In bloom: April – May
Fruit: October
Zelkova is taller and has a thicker trunk than other deciduous broad-leaf trees. In winter, this distinctive tree looks like an upside-down broom. The fresh green leaves in spring and yellow leaves in autumn are a beautiful sight.

●カツラ
花：4～5月 黄葉：10～11月
樹形が整って気品があり、新緑が美しい木です。葉形はハート形で愛らしい印象です。秋に鮮やかに黄葉するなど、年間を通じて楽しめる木です。
Japanese Judas
In bloom: April – May
Yellow leaves: October – November
The tree is elegant, and its fresh green leaves are beautiful. The cute, heart shaped leaves change to vivid yellow in autumn. The tree's changing beauty is a joy throughout the year.

●センダン
花：5～6月 実：10～11月
横に広がるパラソルツリーの樹形で、明るい緑陰をつくり、デッキとの相性も良いこもれびが楽しめる木です。実は野鳥が好んで食べに来ます。
Neem
In bloom: May – June
Fruit: October – November
The tree looks like a parasol. Its leaves provide bright green shade, as the sunlight filters through the foliage onto the deck. Wild birds love its fruit.

●ヒトツバタゴ
花期：5月
白色の花を円錐状に集めて樹冠いっぱいに咲かせる姿は、まるで雪が積もったようで圧巻です。別名ナンジャモンジャノキ。
Chionanthus Retusus
In bloom: May
The white flowers are conical. In full bloom, the beautiful blossoms cover the entire tree like snow.

子ども達の五感を刺激する植栽計画
Planting Plans that Develop Children's Senses

子ども達は五感を使って、木にふれ合うことで、豊かな感性を養います。
Trees develop children's senses.

●花や紅葉が美しく、季節感を感じる木
Trees with beautiful flowers and autumn leaves that show seasonal changes

●食べられる実のなる木
Trees that bear edible fruit

●サルスベリ
花：7～9月
夏に長期間にわたって咲く花は、花弁の縁が縮れ、独特ですが、美しく、よく目立ちます。貴重な夏の花木です。
Crape Myrtle
In bloom: July – September
Crape myrtle blooms in summer, and the blossoms last a long time. The edges of the petals are curled, giving them a beautifully distinctive look.

●コブシ
花：3～4月 実：9～10月
葉に先がけて樹冠に雪が積もったように白い花でおおわれます。秋の赤い集合果も形がおもしろく、握り拳状となるため、この名があります。
Magnolia Kobus
In bloom: March – April
Fruit: September – October
Before its leaves emerge, white flowers bloom to cover the tree like snow. In autumn, red fruit grows in unique clusters that look like a fist. The Japanese name of the tree, "Kobushi," means "fist."

●イロハモミジ
花：4～5月 実：7～9月
秋の紅葉が美しく、最も代表的なカエデです。枝は四方へと斜上し、樹姿に優雅な趣があり、葉は光を通しやすく、こもれびが美しい木です。
Acer Palmatum
In bloom: April – May
Fruit: July – September
The autumn leaves of this common maple are beautiful. The branches spread upward diagonally in four directions. The beautiful sunshine that filters through the foliage of this elegant tree produces a beautiful look.

●ヤマボウシ
花：6～7月 実：9～10月
白い花を多くつけ、紅葉も美しい木です。実はブドウ粒大の集合果で、食べられます。年間を通じて楽しめる木です。
Dogwood
In bloom: June – July
Fruit: September – October
Dogwood produces charming white blossoms, and its autumn leaves are beautiful. It produces grape-size compound fruit that is edible. This tree is a joy throughout the year.

●ヤマモモ
花：3～4月 実：6～7月
細かい葉が枝先に密について整った樹冠をつくる木です。雌雄異株で雌木に赤い実がつき食べられます。果実は生食の他、ジャム、砂糖漬けなどにされます。
Myrica Rubra
In bloom: March – April
Fruit: June – July
Thin leaves on the branches give this tree its beautiful shape. It is dioecious, and the female bears red fruit that is edible fresh from the tree, or it can be made into jam or preserved in sugar.

●香(かおり)の木
Scented Trees

●タイサンボク
花：5〜6月 実：10〜12月
直幹で広円柱状の整った樹形になる木です。光沢のある濃緑色の大きな葉が密生し、花はモクレン科の花らしく、白色大形で芳香があります。

Evergreen Magnolia
In bloom: May – June
Fruit: October – December
This tree has a straight trunk and a beautiful broad cylindrical shape. Its large, shiny dark-green leaves grow thickly, and its large white flowers have the sweet scent common to the magnolia family.

●キンモクセイ
花：9〜10月
よく分枝し刈込にも耐えるため、整形で鐘状形の美しい樹冠になる木です。秋に小さな甘い香りのする小花をたわわにつけます。

Fragrant Olive
In bloom: September – October
Fragrant olive has many branches and can be trimmed to grow into a beautiful bell shape. It bears small sweetly scented flowers in autumn.

それぞれの園庭の規模や環境に配慮した植栽計画の例
Planting plans tailored to the size and environment of individual playgardens

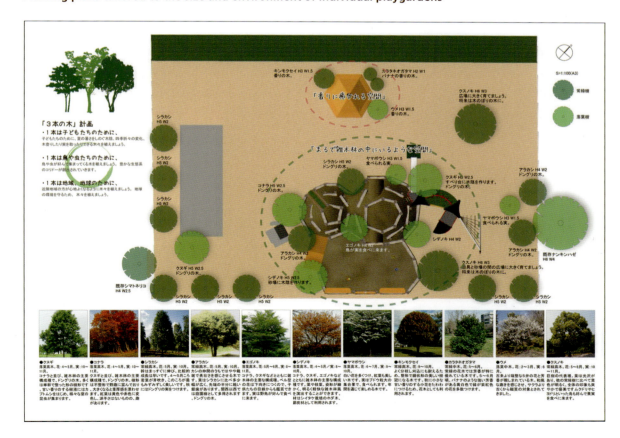

【第3章】園庭を組み立てる

■スカイシェード/SKY Shades

オーストラリアで開発された「スカイシェード」は、室内外を問わず、気温上昇を抑えて紫外線をカットし、快適な空間を実現します。

Developed in Australia, SKY Shades reduce temperature and block UV light both inside and out to produce a comfortable space.

---

①有害な紫外線を90%カット
光、風、雨は適度に通し、紫外線を大幅にカットします。

②夏場の温度上昇を防ぐ
園庭に日陰をつくると、風が吹くと夏場でも涼しく感じます。熱射病の心配も軽減します。エアコン使用量や水まき用途での水道使用量を削減することが可能です。

③腐食・汚れに強く、優れた耐久性能
チタン加工された先進素材（ポリエチレン）の高分子構造と高度な織加工が、腐食に強く、汚れを寄せつけず、高い衝撃吸収性・耐久性・耐摩耗性を発揮します。

④軽量で水洗いができ、取り扱いが容易

⑤スタイリッシュな色とデザイン

(1) Blocks up to 90% of harmful UV light
SKY Shades allow light, wind and rain to penetrate moderately while significantly blocking UV light.

(2) Prevents temperature increase in summer
Providing shade on the playgarden helps children feel cooler when the breeze blows in summer. These shades protect the children from the sun. They also reduce the need for air conditioning and the amount of water needed for plants.

(3) Highly durable and resistant to corrosion and stains
The polymer structure of the advanced material (titanium polyethylene) and the advanced weaving technology realize outstanding resistance to corrosion and stains, and provide shock absorption, durability, and wear resistance.

(4) Light, washable, and easy to handle

(5) Stylish colors and design

紫外線が人体に与える影響について

紫外線曝露率と皮膚癌の発症率には明らかな関連性があります。ある研究所の実験によれば、真夏の1時間/日相当の紫外線を照射し続けた被験体の77%に日光角化症が、そのうち21%に皮膚癌が発症しました。ちなみに同期間に照射をしなかった被験体では、まったく発症しませんでした。また紫外線は人体におけるビタミンDの生成に必要ですが、これは成人の必要量100%を生成するにも日本のほぼ全域で10～30分/日（季節・天候による）の日光照射で十分であることがわかっています。

オーストラリアでは、以前より遊び場には紫外線対策が義務づけられており、日本でも2004年4月、環境省から「紫外線保健指導マニュアル」が発表されました。

※「紫外線保健指導マニュアル」は下記URLより入手可能です。
http://www.env.go.jp/chemi/kenkou.html

Impact of UV light on the human body

UV light exposure is clearly associated with the incidence of skin cancer. According to research, 77% of individuals exposed to the equivalent of 1 hour of UV light per day in summer developed solar keratosis; and 21% of these individuals also developed skin cancer. On the other hand, individuals with zero exposure to UV light were free of UV light-related problems. UV light is, however, needed to produce vitamin D in the human body. For this, 10 to 30 minutes of exposure to UV light per day (depending on season and weather) is sufficient to produce 100% of the required vitamin D for adults in almost every region throughout Japan.
In Australia, every playgarden is required to monitor UV light. In Japan too, the Ministry of the Environment released its UV Light Health Guide in April 2004.

*The Japanese version of the UV Light Health Guide is available on the Ministry of Environment official website at the address shown below:
http://www.env.go.jp/chemi/kenkou.html

仕様/ specification

カラー/ Colors

形状/ Shapes

※A・Bは3か所、C・Dは4か所にDリングがついている／*A and B have a D ring in three locations, and C and D have it in four locations.

立正佼成会附属 佼成育子園／東京都杉並区／
Rissho Koseikai Kosei Ikujien/ Suginami-ku, Tokyo

大森みのり幼稚園／東京都大田区／
Omori Minori Kindergarten/ Ota-ku, Tokyo

■ランダムフェンス／Random Fence

優しくナチュラルな雰囲気をつくり出すウッドフェンスは、外からの視線を遮断し、落ち着いた遊び場をつくります。高さはランダムで向こう側をのぞき込むことができる小窓が開いています。ハンガーポットで植物を飾ることもできます。

Wood fencing produces a gentle, natural atmosphere that separates the area from the outside and creates calm in the playgarden. The height of each board is random, and the fencing features small windows that allows the children to look out onto the other side. Planters can be hung on the wall as well.

向こう側では何が起こってるかな？ 小窓からのぞくのも楽しい遊び／What's up over there? It is also fun to look through the small window.

こもれびデッキと組み合わせると木のぬくもりのあふれた落ち着いた空間になる／Combined with the Sunshine Deck, it becomes a settled space filled with the warmth of wood.

■小さな小屋とみちくさデッキ／Small Hut & Michikusa Deck

草木の豊かな空間にデッキを設けました。中央の木の下に腰かけを用意し、コミュニケーションの場となるようにしました。奥には小さな小屋をつくり、遊びの場としても活用できるようになっています。

A deck can be installed in spaces filled with green. A bench under a tree growing in the middle of the playgarden promotes interaction among the children. A small hut can be installed at the back of the deck to provide children a place to play together.

※デッキ・小屋は敷地の形状に合わせ設計変更できます／*The deck and the hut can be tailored to the space.

【第3章】園庭を組み立てる

■ 水遊び小屋 ／ Water Play Cottage

水遊び小屋は水遊びを充実させるアイテムと組み合わせることができます。砂遊びに水の要素が加わると、子ども達の想像力を刺激し、次々と遊びが発展していきます。ウォーターシーソーやガチャポンプと組み合わせるとさらに楽しい遊びになります。

The cottage can be combined with other water-play items. Adding water to sand promotes imagination, which significantly expands play activities. Combining the cottage with a Water Seesaw or Gacha Pump makes the playgarden even more fun.

左／高床式タイプは小屋の中は子ども達の秘密基地。友達と協力したり、順番待ちのルールを覚える。右／砂庭に設置し、HAGS「クラーノ（蛇口）」を組み合わせた水遊び小屋。／(Left) Inside the raised-floor-style hut is a secret base for children. Cooperating with friends and learning to wait their turn. (Right) A cottage for water play installed in the sand garden and combined with a HAGS tap "CRANO."

■ 高床式どろだんご小屋 ／ Raised-Floor-Style Hut for Mud Ball Making

小屋には砂遊びに便利な作業台や、つくった泥だんごを展示・保管することができる飾り棚があります。さらに、子ども達が自分で砂遊び道具を片づけるための収納棚やシャベル掛けを備えています。小屋のデッキにあるベンチは、子ども達の憩いの空間にもなります。

The hut has a work table that is just right for sand play, and cabinets for the mud balls the children have made. It also has a storage rack for sand play tool cleaning, and hooks for shovels. The bench on the deck provides a space for children to have fun with friends.

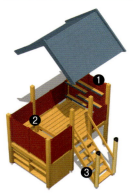

❶ 飾り棚／Cabinet
❷ ベンチ／Bench
❸ 階段／Stairs
❹ 収納棚・シャベル掛け／Storage Rack & Hook for Shovels
❺ 作業台／Work Table

製品サイズ（参考） W2.2 × D1.5 × H2.4m ／ Product Size (Reference): W 2.2 × D 1.5 × H 2.4m

左から／収納棚には道具を置いたり、泥だんごを飾ることも。つくった泥だんごを飾り棚に飾る。作業台で泥だんごづくりに没頭。階段で飾り棚やデッキのある２階へ／(From the Left) Tools can be stored and mud balls can be exhibited in the cabinet. The mud balls that the children have made are exhibited in the cabinet. Children concentrate on making mud balls at the work table. Go to the second level where a cabinet and deck are installed.

■ネットの海／The Net Sea

手足だけでなく、体感（胴体部分）も使って、遊び環境を認識し、自分の身体を自分の意思で自由に動かせる能力を育む新製品です。

This new product nurtures children's ability to more skillfully recognize the environment using their bodies and moving flexibly.

DNA ネット
スタートからゴールまで 90 度回転しながら進む、はしご状の吊り橋です
DNA Net
Children move forward on this net suspension bridge by rotating their body 90 degrees.

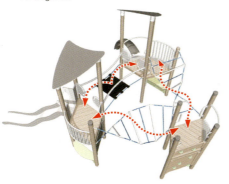

まめのきネット
登り遊びと渡り遊びを融合し、左右に繋がるデッキ間を上下にも左右にも移動できます
Beanstalk Net
This net integrates climbing and crossing activities, which allow children to move freely up and down, left and right between the two decks.

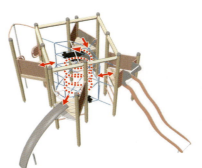

■夢のかけ橋／Bridge of Dreams

遊びの世界へ子ども達を誘う大きなつり橋です。遊び場の凹地の上に架けるのが最適ですが、平地にも架けることができます。通路は高圧真空含浸防腐処理の板からできており、定まった位置にボルトとチェーンで固定されているため、破損してもすぐに取り換えることができます。手すりはプラスチックカバー付きの亜鉛メッキのチェーンで握っても安全です。

The Bridge of Dreams is a large suspension bridge that brings children to activities. It is best to place it over a hollow on the playgarden; however, it can also be installed over level ground. The pathway is made of wooden plates preserved with vacuum pressure impregnation. The wooden plates are fixed with bolts and chain at predetermined locations, which makes it possible to replace them quickly even if the wooden plates are damaged. The handrails are made of galvanized chain with a plastic cover, which is safe for the children.

イメージパース（実際の製品とは異なります。）／Illustration (May differ from actual product.)

遊具接続型
＜必要面積／固定方＞ HAGS ユニプレイに取付
＜製品状態＞ 組み立てキット
＜寸法＞ つり橋の長さ 4.0m（～2.5m）、通路の幅 0.9m。／
Combining with other equipment
<Required Area/ Installation> Installed into HAGS Uniplay
<Assembly> Assembly kit <Size> Length of the suspension bridge: 2.5 – 4.0 m, Width of the pathway: 0.9 m

イメージパース（実際の製品とは異なります。）／Illustration (May differ from actual product.)

独立型
＜必要面積／固定方＞ 20.0 × 4.0m／コンクリート
＜製品状態＞ 組み立てキット
＜寸法＞ つり橋の真ん中部分の標準的な長さ 8.0m、通路の幅 0.9m／
Independent type
<Required Area/ Installation> 20.0 × 4.0 m/ Concrete
<Assembly> Assembly kit <Size> Standard length of the middle of the suspension bridge: 8.0 m, Width of the pathway: 0.9 m

お披露目式
Opening ceremony

何もない場所に一からつくる、既存のものをつくり直すといった工程を経て完成した新しい園庭や遊具たち。子ども達に遊具を紹介するお披露目式では、目を輝かせながら大きな歓声とともに子ども達が遊具で遊ぶ光景を目にすることができます。私たちはこれからもたくさんの感動をみなさんにお届けしていきたいと思っています。

New or refurbished equipment is installed on flat ground. At the opening of the playgarden, we were happy to see the excited children playing on the equipment and shouting with joy. We continue providing the best equipment for individual schools and bringing the excitement of play to everyone.

福井佼成幼稚園
Fukui Kosei Kindergarten

保護者や地域の関係者の方々が集まった園庭見学体験会。広い園庭の至る所で遊んでいる子ども達をみんなで見守る／Parents and residents in the community gathered to see the playgarden, and they watched the excited children playing happily.

浦和みずほ幼稚園
Urawa Mizuho Kindergarten

どのクラスが最初に遊ぶ？先生方による白熱のじゃんけん大会の結果で遊ぶクラスが決まった／Which class gets to play first? A game of rock-paper-scissors decides the big question.

円乗寺保育園
Enjoji Nursery School

新しい園庭を前に落成式。じゃぶじゃぶ池での水遊びで、遊び始めから子ども達も先生もみんなびしょ濡れ／We opened the new playgarden, and everyone got wet playing in the Jabu Jabu Pond.

光明第一保育園
Koumyou Daiichi Nursery School

近所の方もお招きした竣工式。「すてきなえんていありがとう」という嬉しい垂れ幕も飾ってくれた／We invited people from the neighborhood to the completion ceremony. A message from the children was written on a banner. "Thank you for building a nice playgarden."

感謝状や子ども達による園庭のイラストなど、うれしいサプライズも
We got a great surprise: thank-you notes from the children with pictures of the playgarden they had drawn themselves.

技術資料

Technical data

安全な遊び環境づくり／Creating a safe environment for children's activities

子ども達がその力を最大限に発揮するために、遊び環境づくりには安全確保が欠かせません。
なぜなら子ども達はいつでも「今できること」のほんの少し先のチャレンジに挑み続けるからです。
アネビーは、ヨーロッパ安全規格「EN-1176」に準拠し、設計・製造・施工の全工程において遊具の安全性確保に努めています。

It is essential to prioritize safety and functionality when choosing playgarden equipment to maximize growth and development. Children tend to try new activities that are a little more advanced than what they are currently able to do.
Aneby ensures safety in all the processes of design, production, and construction in accordance with the European Standards for Playgarden Equipment EN-1176.

遊びの価値

　子ども達の遊び、中でもとりわけ「挑戦」の要素をもつものは、その「遊びの価値(Play Value)」の一部に少しの危険を含んでいるものが多く存在しています。例えば、登り遊びとは「今居るところよりも高い位置に移動する」遊びのため、おのずと落下の可能性を含んでいることになります。こういった危険に対応する力を培うことで、子ども達はより安全で確実な判断力と身のこなしを体験し、自分の力として習得していくものだと考えられています。この「挑戦」の要素を安全基準上は「リスク」と呼び、子ども達の発達に必要な「遊びの価値」の一部と捉えています。

　しかし遊びの一部を構成する要素である「リスク」に対して、一般的に「あってはならない危険」と呼ばれる危険もあります。これが「ハザード」です。子ども達が正しく結果を予測することが不可能なものや、「事故分析ステージ」(右図)に見られるように失敗したときの身体的損傷が大き過ぎるものを「ハザード」と呼び、安全基準はこの「ハザード」が起こる原因を取り除くことを目的として定められています。

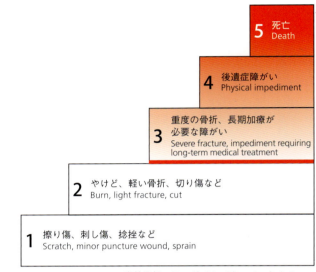

事故分析ステージ／Accident Analysis Stage

Play Value

Activities that are somewhat challenging often include risk. For example, climbing includes the possibility of falling. Developing the ability to handle such risks helps children develop the ability to make safe decisions and movements. The challenging elements are called risks from the perspective of safety standards, and they are considered part of play value as it relates to growth.

While there are risks that should not occur, other risks are an essential part of the activities. The risks that should be alleviated are called hazards, risks that are hard for children to predict, or that may cause significant injury, as shown in the "Accident Analysis Stage (in the right)." The safety standards are specified to remove the causes of such hazards.

リスクとハザード

リスク

リスクは、子ども達の発達にとって必要な危険性であり、冒険や挑戦の要素となる遊びの価値のひとつです。遊びの中で子ども自身が予測し、判断できる危険性がリスクであり、その対応を学び、経験を積み重ねることによって、危険を予測できるようになる重要な要素です。

ハザード

ハザードは、遊びがもっている冒険や挑戦といった遊びの価値とは関係のないところで事故を発生させるおそれのある危険性です。また、子どもが予測できず、どのように判断すれがよいのか判断不可能な危険性もハザードであり、子どもが危険をわからずに行うことは、リスクへの挑戦とはなりません。

Risk & Hazard

Risk

Risk is an essential element in physical and mental development, and an important value in adventurous and challenging activities. Experiencing such risks and learning the proper responses, children learn to predict risks and make proper judgements while playing.

Hazard

Hazard is risk that may cause accidents that have no relation to the adventure or challenges targeted in activities. In addition, risk that children cannot predict is also hazard. If children do not really comprehend the risk and try to do something, it is not a challenge to the risk.

出典：国土交通省『都市公園における遊具の安全確保に関する指針（改訂第2版）』国土交通省 都市・地域整備局公園緑地・景観課, 2014年, P.8／Source: "Guidelines for Maintaining the Safety of Playgarden Equipment in Urban Parks (2nd Revision)" by the Ministry of Land, Infrastructure and Transport (MLIT). Parks, Green Spaces and Landscape Division, City and Regional Development Bureau, MLIT. 2014. P.8

安全規準

遊具は全て「EN-1176」に準拠して設計・生産しています。
「EN-1176」は1977年にドイツが制定開始した「DIN-7926」安全基準を引き継ぎ、世界で最も権威ある基準です。
現在ではEU（ヨーロッパ連合）を中心とした世界33ヶ国で採用され、日本でも2002年の安全基準制定の際に参考としています。

Safety standards

All equipment is designed and manufactured in accordance with EN-1176.
EN-1176 superseded DIN-7926 and represents the most authoritative playgarden equipment standards specified by Germany.
Currently, 33 countries, mainly in the EU, have adopted the standards. Japan used EN-1176 as a reference when safety standards were established in 2002.

EN-1176

遊具製品本体の安全性を規定したものです。

各国の事故レポートから「ハザード」となる寸法や高さ・形状などを分析し、「ハザード」と「リスク」を正しく切り分け、詳細をまとめたものが基準となっています。

基準は8つのカテゴリーに分類され、あらゆる種類の遊具に適応しています。また、新しい形状の遊具にも適応できるように基準は1週間単位で更新されています。

遊具から「遊びの価値（Play Value）」が失われないことを前提とし、遊具の耐久性の確保や遊ぶ利用者の安全を最大限保証しています。

1. 一般的安全対策と試験方法
2. スウィング（ブランコ）
3. スライド（すべり台）
4. 空中ケーブル
5. 回転遊具
6. ロッキング遊具
7. 設置・検査・維持・管理
8. 空間とエリアに対する安全確保の要件と手法

※完全に入退場が管理された場所に設置される遊具は本基準の対象外となります。

EN-1176

EN-1176 specifies the safety requirements for playgarden equipment. Utilizing accident data from different countries, sizes, heights and forms that may cause hazards are analyzed, and the details of hazards and risks are specified.

The standard is categorized into the following eight subjects. In order to respond to new equipment, the standards are updated each week. Considering maintenance of the value of play, EN-1176 ensures the durability of equipment and the safety of users.

1. General safety requirements and test methods
2. Swings
3. Slides
4. Aerial cables
5. Carousels
6. Rocking equipment
7. Installation, inspection, maintenance and operation
8. Specific safety requirements and test methods for spatial networks

*Playgarden equipment installed at locations where the entrance and exit are completely managed are not subject to these standards.

EN-1177

遊具の設置路盤に関する取り決めです。

遊具を設置する際に「EN-1176」と組み合わせて適用され、主に即死と後遺症を防止します。

落下事故による損傷の度合いは落下高さと路盤の衝撃吸収力によって決まるため、設置される遊具の落下高さ(「EN-1176」にて規定)に応じて、HIC(頭部損傷係数)が1,000未満となるような衝撃吸収路盤の整備が求められます。

EN-1177

EN-1177 specifies the requirements for impact absorption playgarden surfacing.
These standards are applied in combination with EN-1176 to prevent death or physical impediment.
The degree of injury by falling is determined by the distance of fall and impact attenuation of the surface. Requirements for the installation of impact-absorbing base material depend on the distance of fall (specified by EN-1176). They set a Head Injury Criterion (HIC) tolerance level of 1,000 as the upper limit for brain injury severity.

運用システム

「EN-1176」は、これを遵守させるための優れた運用システムを持っています。

基準策定委員会と検査機関とは別の組織であり、検査機関のみが検査済マークの認証権限をもちます。そのため不正行為は未然に防止され、検査製品は常に高い安全性が保たれているのです。

Operating System

EN-1176 specifies operating systems to ensure compliance with the standards.
The standardization committee and inspection organization are separated. The inspection organization alone is authorized to provide certification. This prevents dishonesty and ensures a high standard of safety for the inspected products.

TÜV適合マーク／TÜV Certification Mark　　TÜV合格証／TÜV Certificate